the accidental vegetarian

the accidental vegetarian

Delicious food without meat

Simon Rimmer

This book is dedicated to Ali, Flo and Hamish

First published in Great Britain in 2004 by Cassell Illustrated,
This edition produced for The Book People Ltd
Hall Wood Avenue, Haydock, St Helens WA11 9UL

A CIP catalogue record for this book is available from the British Library.

ISBN 1 84403 3236

Photographs by Jason Lowe
Designed by Simon Daley
Edited by Barbara Dixon and Victoria Alers-Hankey

Printed in China

Contents

Introduction

When I bought Greens in 1990 I had two cookery books, a bank loan and no idea how to cook! The plan was that I and Simon Connolly, my business partner, would swan around as the hosts with the most, drinking nice wine and chatting up women while someone else cooked and we coined it in, big-style. That was until we worked out the size of our bank loan and the cost of employing a chef – so we became the chefs.

Simon and I met while working as waiters in the Steak and Kebab restaurant in Manchester. It was a brilliant place to work, full of people waiting to do other things – act, write, fly to the moon – but all loving the buzz of the place. Let me tell you something about the restaurant industry, the hours seem unsociable to you, but there isn't a more sociable job in the world. You work hard, meet great people and then sit down at the end of the shift and have a few bevvies with your mates.

From there I'd got the restaurant bug, so we decided to open our own place. At the time it didn't matter what sort of restaurant it was as long as it was cheap. I had always had my eye on Greens, then one morning I drove past it and saw a 'For Sale' sign being put outside. It was too good to resist and after much negotiation we became the proud owners of a veggie cafe.

I should point out here that we were, and still are, carnivores, so looking through veggie cookbooks in 1990, and being confronted with brown, stodgy food that was all a little bit worthy, was not fun. So we opened with such 'classics' as nut roast, vegetarian lasagne and some dreadful generic curry – you don't have to tell me how awful it sounds.

It was chaos at the start. We had no idea how to organize our preparation and purchasing and we were working 100 hours a week for practically nothing. I hated everything we were cooking, but we were improving.

Surprisingly, we were busy; while the food left a lot to be desired, we were overtly friendly and working very hard. I'd caught the food bug; I was determined to make veggie food more exciting, to get people to eat at Greens because the food was good. I consumed cookery books, learnt techniques, researched cultures who have great vegetarian dishes – Asian, Mediterranean, African – and tried to use French and Italian techniques alongside them; I was extremely experimental and obsessed.

After two years I was getting there; the restaurant was full and the food had become unique. I sourced unusual suppliers of fruit and veg to bring exotics to the table, I looked for different pasta makers and vegetarian cheese suppliers and I made sure that the still popular generic 'vegetable' term never appeared on the menu.

After thirteen years I still love Greens. It feels like home. Our customers are very protective of it, they don't like change, or the fact that they can't always get a table – we reckon we turn away 400 people a week, which is quite amazing, so if you fancy coming, book early!

I think my food is best described as magpie cuisine – I'll steal an idea from anywhere, combining an Asian curry with Jamaican rice and peas. I always try to let the availability of ingredients influence the menus: strawberry soups in summer, Italian bean and Parmesan-roasted parsnips in winter, crisp radish and watercress salads in May.

The recipes in this book are both attainable and inspiring. I don't have formal training as a chef, so I've learnt by the seat of my pants. It hasn't been easy, but it's been a fantastic journey and I'm still learning – so what are you waiting for, turn the pages and get cooking!

Dips and morsels

Feta cheese
bread

There's something really satisfying about making bread – watching it rise, kneading the dough and, best of all, eating warm bread that you've made for yourself. This bread is so delicious, all you need with it is extra-virgin olive oil and some pickled chillies.

1 Dissolve the yeast and sugar in a little of the water. This takes about 5 minutes.

2 Tip the flour and salt onto a work surface and make a well in the centre. Add the rest of the water and the now frothy yeast mix and mix to a dough. Knead for 7–8 minutes until it stops being sticky – the dough is ready when it will stretch out between your hands without breaking.

3 Put the dough into an oiled bowl, cover and leave to double in size – at least 2 hours.

4 Turn the dough out onto a lightly floured surface and 'knock back' – to get all the puffiness out of it.

5 Knead the oil, cheese, mint and pepper into the dough, divide into four pieces and mould each into a round loaf. Put on a buttered and floured baking tray, cover with a damp cloth and leave to rise at room temperature for 40–60 minutes.

6 Preheat the oven to 180ºC/350ºF/mark 4. Glaze the loaves with egg wash and bake for 30–40 minutes. Leave to cool.

15g/½oz instant yeast

1 tsp caster sugar

600ml/1 pint warm water

1kg/2¼lb strong bread flour, plus extra for dusting

2 tbsp salt

4 tbsp extra-virgin olive oil, plus extra for greasing

350g/12oz feta cheese, crumbled

handful of freshly chopped mint leaves

freshly ground black pepper

butter, for greasing

1 egg, beaten, for eggwash

Blinis with soured cream and roasted peppers

Makes 15

The joy of blinis is that they're dead versatile – top them with sweet, savoury or a combination of the two. Have them for breakfast, dinner or tea, make them big or small. Use your imagination for the toppings.

1 First make the blinis. Sift the flours and a little salt into a bowl. Make a well in the centre and add the two whole eggs and one egg white.

2 Mix together the yeast, sugar and milk and leave for a couple of minutes. Pour this slowly into the flour mix and whisk to make a smooth batter. Stir in the butter.

3 Cover the batter and leave in a warm place for 1 hour.

4 Meanwhile, make the topping. Roast or char the peppers until the skin is blackened. Put them in a plastic bag, seal and let them go cold, when the skin will fall away. Deseed the peppers and cut into wide strips.

5 Just before cooking the blinis, whisk the remaining egg white and fold into the batter.

6 Heat a little oil in a frying pan. Pour enough batter into the pan to make a 10cm/4inch blini. When the batter bubbles up, flip it over and cook the other side. Keep the blini warm while you make the rest of the pancakes in the same way.

7 Spoon some soured cream onto each blini and top with some of the pepper pieces, an olive and a twist of black pepper.

225g/8oz buckwheat or wholemeal flour

225g/8oz plain flour

2 whole eggs, plus 2 egg whites

45g/1¾oz fresh yeast

2 tsp caster sugar

700ml/1¼ pints warm milk

1 tbsp melted butter

vegetable oil for frying

salt

For the topping

4 red peppers

225g/8oz set soured cream

15 black Ascoloni olives

freshly ground black pepper

Spicy red pepper humous with coriander seed flat bread

Feeds 6

I thought long and hard about putting humous in the book, it's the kind of thing that you expect from a veggie cookbook – but this is different! Firstly, the humous is lovely and garlicky, it's also lemony and it's got a great little kick at the end from the peppers. Making breads can be hit and miss at times, which is why I love making flat breads – you have a little more margin for error, plus they have a delicious taste and texture.

1 Start with the bread. Dry-fry the coriander seeds, then lightly crush them in a mortar and pestle. Don't turn them into a powder, but also don't leave them tooth-breaking size. Put them into a pan with the water and bring just to the boil.

2 Put the yoghurt into a bowl and add the yeast. Pour the coriander seeds and water into the bowl and stir well.

3 Add 200g/7oz of the flour, and use your hands to combine it well, then cover the bowl and leave to prove for 25 minutes. Contrary to popular belief, it doesn't have to be somewhere warm, but it helps.

4 After the proving, turn the dough out onto a lightly floured surface, add the salt, oil and remaining flour and give this a really good mix. Put back in the bowl, cover and leave to prove again for 1 hour, when it should have just about doubled in size.

5 Turn the dough out onto a lightly floured surface and knock it back. Divide the dough into six, then roll into little balls. Roll each ball out to 10–12.5cm/4–5inch circles.

6 To cook the bread, brush each circle of dough with a little oil and cook for about 30 seconds on each side, either in a shallow pan or on a griddle pan. Put a cooked flat bread on each plate.

7 For the humous, put all the ingredients except the oil, olives and chilli in the blender and whiz until smooth. With the motor running, add a stream of oil to loosen the mixture. Turn out into a dish, garnish with the olives and chargrilled chilli and serve with the coriander seed flat bread.

400g/14oz tinned chick peas, drained and rinsed

4 garlic cloves

50g/2oz tahini paste

juice of 3 lemons

100g/3½oz Pepperdew spicy red peppers, or sweet pickled chilli peppers

olive oil to loosen

salt and freshly ground black pepper

6 olives and 1 red chilli, charred or griddled, to serve

For the coriander seed flat bread

1 tsp coriander seeds

100ml/3½fl oz water

250ml/9fl oz natural yoghurt

1½ tsp dried yeast

550g/1¼lb strong plain flour, plus extra for dusting

1 tbsp salt

2 tbsp vegetable oil, plus extra for brushing

Fried halloumi with lemon and capers

Feeds 4

You'll not see halloumi on a cheeseboard, because raw it tastes a bit like plastic, but when dusted with spiced flour and fried it becomes a right tasty morsel. After that the zingy lemon dressing cuts through the sweetness of the cheese to perfection. Mop up the dressing with my feta cheese bread (see page 10), or a slab of crusty white if that's what you've got.

1 Combine the flour with the cayenne and season well. Dust each slice of cheese with the flour.

2 Heat some oil in a pan until hot, then fry the halloumi for about 1 minute on each side, until golden.

3 To make the dressing, put the lemon juice, vinegar, garlic and mustard into a bowl and whisk together. Keep whisking and slowly add the oil, a little at a time. Season to taste, then add the capers and herbs.

4 Sit two pieces of cheese on each plate (it looks good on top of some peppery watercress) and drizzle with the dressing.

25g/1oz plain flour
1 tsp cayenne pepper
225g/8oz halloumi cheese, cut into 8 slices
vegetable oil for frying
salt and freshly ground black pepper
watercress, to serve (optional)

For the dressing

juice of 1 lemon
1 tbsp white wine vinegar
1 garlic clove, crushed
1 tsp Dijon mustard
3 tbsp extra-virgin olive oil
1½ tsp capers in vinegar
freshly chopped parsley
freshly chopped coriander leaves

Sticky rice and peanut balls

Feeds – well it depends on
how many beers

The ultimate beer snack. Be very careful, these little beasts are addictive: Thai spices, peanuts, rice and deep-fried – they're crying out for a beer.

1 Blend half the rice in a food processor until it's not quite a paste. Turn out into a bowl and combine this with the remaining rice, the curry paste, lime juice and salt to taste. Mix it up really well.

2 Roll the mixture into balls 2.5–4cm/1–1½inches in diameter. Now roll the balls in the peanuts and deep-fry in hot oil until golden. Drain on kitchen paper and serve with chilli sauce.

400g/14oz cooked Thai jasmine rice

4 tbsp red Thai curry paste

juice of 1 lime

150g/5½oz roasted peanuts, finely crushed

vegetable oil for deep-frying

salt

sweet chilli sauce for dipping

Favetta

Feeds 4

This is such a lovely dish whether you are a veggie or not. You can use frozen beans, but fresh ones are so much better. Serve with coriander seed flat bread (see page 12) or with some roasted vegetables.

1 Blanch the beans in boiling water for 2 minutes, maximum, then plunge into really ice-cold water. Drain the beans and peel off the hard outer skins.

2 Put the beans, thyme, garlic and lemon juice in a blender and pulse until smooth.

3 With the motor running, pour in the oil and blend until it's the consistency of humous.

4 Turn out into a bowl and season.

400g/14oz fresh broad beans

handful of fresh thyme

1 garlic clove

juice of 1 lemon

100ml/3½fl oz extra-virgin olive oil

salt and freshly ground black pepper

Tomato and mozzarella cakes

Feeds 6

Each cake is a tomato risotto filled with melting cheese. You may have eaten the little round versions of these called 'arancini', or little oranges. These larger versions could make a great lunch with simply dressed rocket.

1 Melt the butter in a heavy-based pan. Add the rice and cook for a couple of minutes on a low heat. When the rice starts to become a little translucent around the edges, add the wine and cook for another minute.

2 Add a ladleful of warm stock (it must be warm to enable the rice to cook properly). When the stock has been absorbed, add another ladleful and continue doing this until all the stock has been added and/or the rice is tender.

3 Next, fold in the sun-dried tomatoes and the cream and season well. Leave the rice to cool.

4 Divide the rice into six and roll into balls. The rice will be nice and sticky. Make a hole in the centre of each ball and press some of the cheese into it. Cover with the rice and flatten into a patty shape.

5 Roll the patties in flour, then egg, then breadcrumbs and deep-fry at 180ºC/350ºF. You don't want the oil to be too hot or the outside will cook and the middle will be cold. Fry till crisp and golden, then drain on kitchen paper and serve with dressed rocket leaves.

50g/2oz butter

450g/1lb arborio rice, rinsed and drained

splash of white wine

850ml/1½ pints warm stock

100g/3½oz sun-dried tomatoes, chopped

splash of cream

150g/5½oz mozzarella cheese, cubed

plain flour for rolling

1 egg, beaten

150g/5½oz fresh breadcrumbs

vegetable oil for deep-frying

dressed rocket leaves, to serve

Thai spiced potato cakes
with spicy coleslaw

Makes 8 cakes

I first went to Thailand in 1996 and I found it so inspiring – it's a food lover's delight. I'd always loved Thai food – green curries, pad-thai, sticky rice – with all their beautiful fragrances. When you're there, the smell of lime leaves, lemon grass, coconut and charring chillies you get from the excellent street food stalls is overwhelming. So this fantastic little morsel will give you a spicy, fragrant taste of the East. If you can't get fresh lime leaves, then use dried, but the smell of fresh makes it worth a trail around the shops. You should have tingly lips from the chillies and the wasabi in the coleslaw – don't go easy on them, live on the edge.

1 First, make the potato cakes. Put the mashed and grated spuds in a large bowl, add all the other potato cake ingredients and season.

2 Mould the mixture into eight 7.5cm/3inch rounds, about 2.5cm/1inch thick (or make sixteen mini-cakes – great for parties), and pop them into the fridge for about 1 hour.

3 Set up three plates or bowls: one with flour, one with eggwash and one with the breadcrumbs. First roll the cakes in flour, dust off any excess, then roll them in the egg and finally in the breadcrumbs.

4 You can shallow- or deep-fry them (I find that deep-frying gives a crisper texture). If you shallow-fry, be careful not to burn them – a gentle heat is best. Either way, they're done when crisp and golden.

5 Put a spoonful of coleslaw on each plate and sit a potato cake on top. Sprinkle some chopped coriander over and add a wedge of lime on the side – and don't forget to pour yourself a nice cold glass of Singha beer.

plain flour, for rolling

2 eggs, beaten, for eggwash

150g/5½oz fresh breadcrumbs

vegetable oil for frying

1 quantity spicy coleslaw, to serve (see page 32)

freshly chopped coriander leaves and lime wedges, to serve

For the potato cakes

3 large Maris Piper potatoes, peeled, cooked and mashed

1 raw potato, peeled and grated

3 tbsp mayonnaise

1 bunch of spring onions, finely chopped

2 small red chillies, deseeded and chopped

freshly chopped coriander leaves

2 garlic cloves, crushed

2 stalks of lemon grass, finely chopped

4 kaffir lime leaves, finely chopped

2.5cm/1inch piece of fresh ginger, finely chopped

1 tsp cinnamon

2 shallots, finely chopped

salt and freshly ground black pepper

Norimaki sushi rolls

Hands up if you thought 'sushi' meant raw fish? Quite a lot of you I reckon. Well, I did too, but it actually means vinegared rice, so with that piece of knowledge you can make these delicious, healthy nori rolls and show off to friends and family about the true meaning of sushi. Nori is roasted and rolled seaweed and comes in sheets.

1 Put the rice in a pan with the water and bring to the boil. Cover and simmer for 5 minutes, then take off the heat, leave covered and allow to cool.

2 When the rice is cool, put it in a bowl, season and add the sugar and vinegar. Mix well.

3 Lay out the nori sheets and spread a little wasabi on each. Put a line, about 2.5cm/1inch wide, of rice a little way in from the bottom edge.

4 Press some cucumber and pepper into the rice. Top with more rice and roll up tightly. Chill for 30 minutes, then cut into 4cm/1½inch long pieces. Cut off and discard the uneven ends.

5 Make a dipping sauce by heating the vinegar, sugar and chilli until the sugar dissolves.

6 Serve the sushi rolls with the dipping sauce, extra wasabi paste, soy sauce and pickled red ginger.

150g/5½oz sushi rice, rinsed thoroughly and drained

225ml/8fl oz water

25g/1oz sugar

50ml/2fl oz rice wine vinegar

4 sheets dried nori

wasabi paste

½ cucumber, peeled, deseeded and cut into batons

½ red pepper, deseeded and cut into batons

salt

soy sauce and pickled red ginger, to serve

For the dipping sauce

100ml/3½fl oz rice vinegar

75g/3oz sugar

1 small red chilli, finely chopped

Patatas bravas

In Spain these are made by deep-frying the potatoes, salting them and squeezing a spicy tomato 'ketchup' over them. But this is the yummiest way to do it – slowly roasting the potatoes with chilli. I like to make them a day in advance so the olive oil, chilli and tomatoes can really get to work on the potato. Whenever we have a party at home I make a bucket-load of these – they do go so well with a cold beer.

1 Preheat the oven to 220ºC/425ºF/mark 7. Heat a load of oil in a massive roasting tin until really hot. Cut the potatoes into 2.5cm/1inch cubes. Chuck away any uneven bits, so you're left with neat shapes, they look nicer.

2 Throw the spuds in the oil and give them a little shake. Season well, then pop into the oven for about 10 minutes until they begin to brown.

3 Add the tomatoes, chillies and garlic and stir well. Cook for another 25–35 minutes until the potatoes are soft on the inside, but with a little bit of crispness outside.

4 Either add the parsley and serve, or leave them until the next day, then reheat, adding more oil, and add the parsley before eating.

5 If you're making these for a party, put a load in a secret place for yourself, you know it makes sense.

lots of olive oil

600g/1lb 5oz Maris Piper, Desiree or King Edwards potatoes, peeled

400g tin of chopped tomatoes

3 red chillies, chopped

4 garlic cloves, crushed

lots of freshly chopped parsley

salt and freshly ground black pepper

Dolmades

Whenever I'm in Greece I can't stop eating these little fellas. There's loads of different varieties – meaty, herby, veggie and these, which have sultanas and pine nuts. Serving them with yummy tzatziki is essential.

1 Heat the oil in a pan and fry the shallots and garlic until soft. Add the rice, sultanas, pine nuts and lemon juice and fry for 1 minute. Season, then add the water.

2 Cover the pan and simmer for 15 minutes, then turn off the heat and leave to cool.

3 Once the mixture is cool, add the spring onions, mint and parsley.

4 Rinse the vine leaves in water, then place them shiny side down on a board. Put about 2 tsp of the cooled stuffing on each leaf and roll into a tight parcel. Chill until ready to eat.

5 For the tzatziki, mix the cucumber with the yoghurt, garlic, mint, lemon juice and seasoning. Tip into a serving bowl and top with a dash of olive oil.

6 You can serve the dolmades either cold or warm (just heat them in a steamer). Put them on a large plate with the tzatziki in the middle and get stuck in.

1 tbsp olive oil

3 shallots, finely chopped

2 garlic cloves, crushed

125g/4½oz short-grain rice, rinsed and drained

50g/2oz sultanas

50g/2oz pine nuts, toasted

juice of 1 lemon

175ml/6fl oz water

1 bunch of spring onions, finely chopped

handful of finely chopped fresh mint leaves and parsley

20 preserved vine leaves

salt and freshly ground black pepper

For the tzatziki

1 cucumber, peeled, deseeded and coarsely grated

200ml/7fl oz Greek yoghurt

4 garlic cloves, crushed

handful of freshly chopped mint leaves

juice of ½ lemon

extra-virgin olive oil

Salads

Santa fé Caesar salad

A good Caesar salad is a joy to behold, but unfortunately the rise of café bars has meant that a bit of cos lettuce, soggy croûtons, mayo and Parmesan are masquerading as the real thing. So here is a great salad, which has the strength of a Caesar with spicy bits of the Mexican border. Hail Caesar-Gringo!

1 To make the dressing, put the mayonnaise, mustard and garlic into a bowl and whisk in the lime juice and vinegar. Mix in the grated Parmesan and season to taste.

2 To make up the salad, cut the cos lettuce into 2.5–5cm/1–2inch wide slices, chuck away the bottom, and put the slices into a large bowl. Season with a little salt and pepper.

3 To make the croûtons, dry-fry the tortillas in a pan until a little charred, then break up into the lettuce bowl.

4 Chuck in the beans and chillies.

5 Add about half the dressing and toss, then add the rest (if you think it's dressed enough with half that's fine) and the avocado, shallots and coriander leaves.

6 Finally, top with some large Parmesan shavings (use a potato peeler to get the right effect) and serve.

1 cos lettuce, trimmed

2 soft corn tortillas

150g/5½oz cooked/tinned pinto beans, or kidney beans, drained and rinsed

2 red chillies, deseeded and chopped

1 ripe avocado, chopped

2 shallots, finely sliced

fresh coriander leaves

salt and freshly ground black pepper

For the dressing

225g/8oz mayonnaise

2 tbsp Dijon mustard

1 garlic clove, crushed

juice of 1 lime

2 tbsp white wine vinegar

100g/3½oz freshly grated Parmesan cheese, plus extra Parmesan to shave for garnish

Sun-blush Niçoise

This is sunshine on a plate – sun-blushed tomatoes, light little gem lettuce, olives and a gorgeous creamy Italian dressing. It's a brilliant starter, because it doesn't fill you up too much, but really gets the juices flowing for more tastes. You'll need some foccacia to mop up the irresistible dressing.

1 Break up the lettuces and divide between six bowls or plates.

2 Toss together the spuds, beans and capers with a little seasoning, then divide them between the bowls.

3 To make the dressing, whiz the egg yolks in a blender, then add the sugar, mustard and seasoning and whiz to combine. With the blender on, slowly add the oil. With the motor still running, slowly add the vinegar. Finally, squeeze in the lemon juice and add the oregano.

4 Spoon a little of the dressing over each salad, then sit an egg half, some sun-blushed tomatoes and olives on top or arrange them around the sides of the bowl.

2 little gem lettuces

200g/7oz boiled small new potatoes

200g/7oz cooked fine beans

100g/3½oz capers in vinegar

3 hard-boiled eggs, halved

150g/5½oz sun-blushed tomatoes

18 large green olives

salt and freshly ground black pepper

For the Italian dressing – makes 1 litre/1¾ pints

4 egg yolks

4 tsp caster sugar

4 tsp Dijon mustard

600ml/1 pint olive oil

200ml/7fl oz white wine vinegar

juice of 3 lemons

freshly chopped oregano leaves

Panzanella

Feeds 6-ish

I did some filming in Tuscany a couple of years ago and ended up doing an impromptu cookery demonstration at a wonderful cookery school near Lucca. After I'd finished, about 20 of us sat down and ate some fantastic pasta and fish, but the highlight was the panzanella, which is really just a pepper, tomato and stale bread salad, but using the juice from the tomatoes and the peppery olive oil from the olive groves at the school made it one of my most memorable meals.

1 Skin the tomatoes by putting a cross on the bottom, plunging them into boiling water for about 30 seconds, then into iced water. The skins will peel off easily. Cut them into quarters, scoop out the seeds into a sieve and press to release the juice into a bowl. Put the quarters into a separate bowl.

2 Skin all the peppers by either grilling them, or roasting them until black. Put them in a plastic bag until cool – the skins will fall off. Then deseed them and cut each into about eight pieces. Put in the bowl with the tomato quarters, then add the chilli, capers and olives.

3 Tear the bread into big chunks and put in a separate bowl.

4 Add the vinegar, garlic and oil to the tomato juice, season and whisk well, then pour over the bread and leave for about 1 hour.

5 Finally, gently combine the tomatoes and peppers mixture with the bread and dressing, and garnish with basil leaves.

6 Pretend you're in Tuscany.

1kg/2¼lb plum tomatoes

2 red peppers

2 yellow peppers (you can use green, but they're a little bitter)

1 small red chilli, deseeded and chopped

100g/3½oz capers, in vinegar or salt

12 large Ascoloni olives – should be black, but I don't like them so I use green

1 ciabatta loaf, preferably stale

4 tbsp red wine vinegar

5 garlic cloves, crushed

about 250ml/9fl oz extra-virgin olive oil, preferably Tuscan

salt and freshly ground black pepper

handful of fresh basil leaves, roughly torn, to garnish

Warm stack of Greek salad with parsley pesto

Feeds 6

A delicious lunch recipe that looks good and yet is simplicity itself. While I say it's Greek, the Italians do help out a bit.

1 Skin the tomatoes by putting a cross on the bottom, plunging them into boiling water for about 30 seconds, then dropping into iced water – the skins will peel off easily. Then slice them to the thickness of a pound coin.

2 Slice the courgettes to the same thickness, season and griddle on both sides until they're nicely striped.

3 To make the pesto, put the garlic and parsley in a blender and whiz together, then with the motor still running add the nuts, cheese and oil. Taste and season.

4 To assemble, you'll need six 10cm/4inch diameter serving rings (or two rings and repeat three times). Sit the rings on a baking tray. Plonk a layer of tomato in the bottom of each ring. (If you're using plum tomatoes, make sure the base is well covered.) Season, then spoon on a little pesto and top with a couple of basil leaves and a layer of sliced or crumbled feta. Repeat with a layer of courgette slices. Then repeat the layering, finishing with a layer of feta.

5 Preheat the oven to 180°C/350°F/mark 4. Drizzle the stacks with a little oil and cook in the oven for 10–12 minutes to warm through. You can flash them under a hot grill to brown, if you want.

6 Unmould each stack onto a plate, and arrange the olives around. Garnish with basil, a good drizzle of oil and a lemon wedge.

6 beef tomatoes, or 12–15 decent-sized plum tomatoes

450g/1lb courgettes

handful of fresh basil leaves, plus extra for garnish

450g/1lb Greek feta cheese

olive oil for griddling and drizzling

18 large Kalamata black olives

lemon wedges, to serve

salt and freshly ground black pepper

For the parsley pesto

2 garlic cloves

large handful of roughly chopped fresh parsley

25g/1oz pine nuts

50g/2oz freshly grated Parmesan cheese

150ml/5fl oz extra-virgin olive oil, Greek of course

Coronation chick peas and potato salad

Feeds 8

I used to think coronation chicken was really naff – it probably still is, but I love it. Well, it set me thinking; why didn't ER2 get anything created for veggies? So by Royal Appointment, here is something for us.

1 Cook the spuds and, while they're still hot, cut into quarters and put in a bowl with the onions and vinaigrette. Toss them well (the spuds will absorb the dressing) and season. Leave to cool.

2 Mix the mayo with the curry paste, then stir into the cooled spuds with the chick peas, sultanas and almonds. Garnish with coriander leaves.

800g/1lb 12oz new spuds, scrubbed

bunch of spring onions, finely chopped

2 tbsp vinaigrette

300ml/10fl oz mayo

50g/2oz smooth curry paste (maybe softened in a little hot water)

100g/3½oz tinned chick peas, drained and rinsed

1 tbsp sultanas

1 tbsp flaked, toasted almonds

salt and freshly ground black pepper

fresh coriander leaves, to garnish

Asparagus, potato and fennel salad with Italian dressing

Feeds 4

I love dishes that include a bit of leftover grub – roasties in this case – and teamed with 'posh' ingredients such as asparagus. Slap a bit of tangy Italian dressing over the top and it makes a brilliant lunch salad or starter.

Slice the asparagus diagonally, cut up the spuds, if necessary, and put all the salad ingredients into a large bowl. Season well and dress with about 200ml/7fl oz of the dressing. (If you like, you can serve this with warm spuds and asparagus.)

12 cooked asparagus spears

about 20 roast spuds

2 shallots, sliced

handful of rocket leaves

1 fennel bulb, blanched and finely sliced

1 quantity of Italian dressing (see page 25)

Pickled cucumber salad

Feeds 4

This is dead easy – a lovely sweetish pickle that gives a great lift to any Oriental dish or tired salad. The warm, fragrant Szechuan peppercorns really add to the dish, but if you can't get them use black ones.

1 Toss the cucumber batons in the salt and put in a colander for about 20 minutes to get rid of excess moisture. Meanwhile, dry-fry the peppercorns for 2–3 minutes until fragrant, then roughly grind in a mortar and pestle.

2 Heat the ground nut and chilli oils in a small saucepan, add the garlic and chilli and cook gently for 2 minutes. Add the sugar and vinegar and simmer until the sugar has dissolved and the mixture is a little syrupy. Rinse and dry the cucumber and add to the pan with the onions. Crank the heat up and count slowly to 10. Take off the heat, let it cool and serve with whatever you fancy – pie, salad, quiche, Chinese.

4 cucumbers, peeled, deseeded and cut into 5cm/2inch long batons

1 tsp salt

2 tbsp Szechuan peppercorns

2 tsp ground nut oil

1 tsp chilli oil

1 garlic clove, crushed

1 small red chilli, deseeded and finely chopped

25g/1oz sugar

2 tbsp rice wine vinegar

2 spring onions, finely chopped

Sweet potato salad

I do love rocket and Parmesan salad, but rocket deserves more, so I grant the rocket the company of sweet potato and mint.

1 Brush the potato slices with the chilli oil and season, then griddle for a couple of minutes on each side.

2 To make the dressing, simply whisk everything together in a small bowl.

3 Put the mint, rocket and shallots into a serving bowl, pour over the dressing and toss gently, then sit the sweet spuds on top.

400g/14oz golden sweet potato, peeled and thinly sliced

chilli oil

handful of fresh mint leaves

200g/7oz fresh rocket leaves

4 shallots, finely sliced

salt and freshly ground black pepper

For the dressing

1 red chilli, deseeded and finely chopped

2 tbsp light soy sauce

juice of 1–2 limes

1tsp caster sugar

Spicy coleslaw

Feeds 2–4

Wasabi is hot green horseradish – it's seriously fiery, but very addictive.

Put the cabbage, onion and carrots into a large bowl and season well. Add the mayo, wasabi and lime leaves and mix it up well.

100g/3½oz red cabbage, finely sliced

½ red onion, finely sliced

2 carrots, grated

50g/2oz mayonnaise

1 tbsp wasabi paste

3 lime leaves, shredded

salt and freshly ground black pepper

Fattoush

I think that Middle Eastern cuisine has some of the best veggie dishes and ingredients on the planet – tabbouleh, kibbeh, borak – all great names and tastes (if you don't know what they are, that can be your homework for next time). I also love the fresh, clean tastes they do so well – this brilliant Lebanese salad is ideal for a summer's day, it's crunchy, zesty and the dressing is divine. Sumac is a dried, crushed berry and it tastes a bit of a cross between cumin and cranberry.

1 To make the dressing, simply whisk all the ingredients together in a bowl.

2 For the salad – again, dead easy – just put all the ingredients in a large bowl and season.

3 Pour the dressing over the salad and gently toss together. I love serving it in a huge bowl and letting everyone pile in.

1 pitta bread, torn into small pieces

8 plum tomatoes, deseeded and quartered

½ cucumber, peeled and cut into batons

½ green pepper cut into strips

8 radishes, sliced

1 shallot, sliced

a few rocket leaves

1 small little gem lettuce

handful of fresh mint leaves

For the dressing

300ml/10fl oz olive oil

juice and zest of 5 lemons

1 garlic clove, crushed

4 tbsp ground sumac

salt and freshly ground black pepper

Griddled aubergine salad
with nuoc cham

Feeds 6

This works brilliantly as a side dish for spicy dishes, but I think it also works as a starter. Beware of this Vietnamese dressing, it is HOT, so make use of the yoghurt.

1 Put the aubergines into a bowl, add a little oil and the lime juice and season with plenty of salt. Toss well.

2 Next, griddle the aubergines in a hot pan until charred. Put to one side.

3 To make the nuoc cham, simply combine all the ingredients in a processor. (I tend to process the dry ingredients first to make it smooth.)

4 Next, dry-fry the cumin seeds until fragrant, then crush them in a mortar and pestle and combine with the yoghurt.

5 Arrange the aubergines on plates, spoon some nuoc cham dressing over and top with the yoghurt.

4 aubergines, cut into wedges, or chunks if large
vegetable oil for griddling
juice of 1 lime
1 tbsp cumin seeds
100ml/3½fl oz natural yoghurt
salt

For the nuoc cham

10 small red chillies
5 garlic cloves
juice of 5 lemons
5 tbsp rice wine vinegar
5 tbsp water

Watermelon salad

This is a great summer dish, making use of juicy watermelon, feta cheese and the spicy bread. I can feel the sun on my body already.

1 Combine all the ingredients for the dressing in a bowl.

2 Toss the salad ingredients in the dressing, season lightly, then sit some of the salad in a good high mound on top of a piece of coriander seed flat bread (see page 12).

200g/7oz Greek feta cheese, cut into 2.5cm/1inch cubes

½ cucumber, deseeded and cut into 5cm/2inch batons

6–8 fresh basil leaves

6 wedges of watermelon, about 75g/3oz each

For the dressing

125ml/4fl oz Greek yoghurt

lots of freshly chopped mint leaves

juice of 1 lime

salt and freshly ground black pepper

Rocket, fig and pecan salad with creamy Lancashire Blue

This is one of the most delicious ways of eating figs. Traditionally you'd probably expect Roquefort or Dolcelatte, but I'm a champion of local produce, so luscious Lancashire Blue it is.

1 Whisk together the oils and vinegar and season well.

2 Put all the remaining ingredients into a large bowl, pour in the dressing, toss together and serve.

2 tbsp walnut oil

1 tbsp vegetable oil

1½ tbsp raspberry vinegar

250g/9oz rocket leaves

½ fennel bulb, very finely sliced

6–8 ripe figs, quartered

150g/5½oz creamy Lancashire Blue, broken into bite-sized cubes

100g/3½oz pecan halves

salt and freshly ground black pepper

Green papaya salad

Feeds 4

I used to eat this hot, spicy salad every day on the beaches on Koh Samui. It's one of those Thai dishes that makes your eyes water and you crave liquid. But take the pain and nibble on raw white cabbage to quell the fire, although ice-cold lager does work well.

1 Put the garlic, shallot and salt to taste in a large mortar and pestle and grind to a paste. Put the paste in a large serving bowl.

2 Coarsely grate the papaya and add to the bowl with the chillies, tomatoes, beans, nuts, lime juice and sugar.

3 Garnish with coriander leaves and lime wedges and serve.

4 garlic cloves

1 shallot, sliced

1 green papaya, peeled and deseeded

3 bird's eye red chillies, deseeded and chopped

2 tomatoes, deseeded and cut into strips

3 raw fine beans, cut into strips

25g/1oz roasted peanuts, crushed

juice of 1 lime

pinch of sugar

sea salt

fresh coriander leaves, to garnish

lime wedges, to serve

Lemon, fennel and oyster mushroom salad

Feeds 4

There's something quite sexy about this salad; maybe it's the lemon marinade combined with the juicy mushrooms and fennel, or maybe it's the way the sauce dribbles down your chin…

1 Trim off the fennel tops, cut the fennel in half lengthways, or quarters if they're large. Blanch in boiling water for about 1 minute, then plunge into ice-cold water. Drain when cool.

2 Whisk together the oil, lemon juice, zest and garlic.

3 Arrange the mushrooms and fennel in a serving dish and season well, then pour over the oil marinade. Add enough oil to just cover the ingredients. Cover and chill for at least 24 hours, then serve with warm foccacia bread to dip into the sauce.

3 fennel bulbs

lots of extra-virgin olive oil

juice and zest of 3 lemons

2 garlic cloves, sliced

200g/7oz oyster mushrooms

salt and freshly ground black pepper

Small platefuls

Aubergine 'roll-mops'

Feeds 4

I love roll-mop herrings, they remind me of my dad, as we're the only members of my family who like them. I created this aubergine version almost as a joke, but I found that everyone loved them, so now you can make them. You really need to pickle the onions for at least a week, otherwise you'll be gurning as you eat. If you want to make this more substantial serve with cold boiled spuds, hard-boiled eggs and fine beans.

1 To pickle the onions, put all the ingredients except the onions in a saucepan and bring to a slow boil. Simmer for 15 minutes, then allow to cool. Pack the onions into a sterilised sealable jar and pour the spiced vinegar over them. Seal the jar and leave for at least 1 week.

2 To assemble the dish, cut the aubergines into strips about the thickness of a pound coin. Season them, then brush with the oil and cook on a griddle for a minute or so each side until nicely striped.

3 Put a little bit of pickled onion (make sure you don't have any seeds in there) at the end of a slice of aubergine, roll it up tightly and secure with a cocktail stick. When you've rolled them all up pour a little more vinegar over and chill for about 20 minutes.

4 Make a dressing by whisking the chopped chives into the cream.

5 Sit a couple of roll-mops on a little watercress and top with a big dollop of the chive cream.

3 large aubergines, topped and tailed
olive oil for brushing
white vinegar for drizzling
freshly chopped chives
200g/7oz soured cream
salt and freshly ground black pepper
watercress, to serve

For the pickled onions

1 litre/1¾ pints white vinegar
1 cinnamon stick
6 cloves
1 tbsp coriander seeds
1 tsp mustard seeds
2 bay leaves
2 red chillies
1 tsp black peppercorns
2 tbsp caster sugar
1½ tbsp salt
2 onions, finely sliced

Aubergine tikka

Feeds 6

This might seem like a bit of a hassle for lunch, but it is worth it and even though there are a lot of ingredients it's easy to prepare. The end result is fantastic, ideal for outdoor summery lunches with friends.

1 Toss the aubergines in oil and salt, then cook on a hot griddle pan on each side until striped.

2 Put all the marinade ingredients into a large bowl and stir to mix. Coat the aubergines well with the marinade, thread onto wooden skewers and put into a dish, then cover and chill for at least 2 hours.

3 To make the coleslaw, simply combine all the ingredients in a bowl.

4 Cook the aubergines under a hot grill, basting with the butter and lemon juice and turning when golden.

5 Serve the aubergine kebabs with a few chillies, lime wedges and the coleslaw.

4–6 aubergines, about 900g/2lb, topped, tailed and cut into chunks
vegetable oil
50ml/2fl oz melted butter
juice of 1 lemon
salt
chillies and lime wedges, to serve

For the marinade

100ml/3½fl oz natural yoghurt
juice of 1 lime
2 garlic cloves, crushed
2.5cm/1inch piece of fresh ginger, finely chopped
1 tbsp ground coriander
1 tsp ground cumin
1 tsp garam masala
1 tsp paprika

For the coleslaw

200ml/7fl oz yoghurt
juice of 2 limes
pinch of cayenne pepper
175g/6oz shredded white cabbage
1 each of red, yellow and orange pepper
10 spring onions, chopped
handful of freshly chopped coriander leaves and stems
1 tbsp ground cumin
1 garlic clove, crushed

Aubergine butty with pesto

Feeds 4

Imagine yourself in Florence with the beauty of the city, the fine ice cream and brilliant small restaurants knocking out exquisite Italian fare – then imagine a Scouser has opened a butty shop using all these influences, that's what this is all about.

1 Preheat the oven to 200ºC/400ºF/mark 6. To make the pesto, put the basil and a little of the oil in a food processor and blitz to make a paste. Add the garlic, pine nuts and Parmesan and blitz with enough oil to make a rich, thick sauce. Turn out into a dish, check the seasoning and keep the pesto cool.

2 Season the aubergines well and toss in oil, then cook on a hot griddle pan on both sides until striped. Do the same with the bread.

3 To assemble the dish, put four rings (about 10cm/4inches wide x 5cm/2inches deep) on a baking sheet and brush a little oil around the inside of each.

4 Press some aubergine into the bottom to form a solid base, then add a slice of tomato and a spoonful of pesto. Then it's a piece of bread, a little oil and mozzarella. Continue layering and finish with a layer of cheese. Drizzle with oil, then cook in the oven for 10–15 minutes until warmed through. Finish off under a hot grill to brown the cheese before serving.

5 Sit each ring on a plate, run a knife around the inside edge and carefully remove the ring. Garnish with a little dressed rocket.

3–4 good-sized aubergines, topped, tailed and sliced into 1cm/½inch discs

vegetable oil for griddling and brushing

1 ciabatta, cut into slices about the thickness of a pound coin

250g/9oz beef tomatoes, thinly sliced

300g/10½oz buffalo mozzarella cheese, thinly sliced

dressed rocket leaves, to garnish

For the pesto

300g/10½oz fresh basil, stalks and leaves

125ml/4½fl oz extra-virgin olive oil

2 garlic cloves

50g/2oz toasted pine nuts

100g/3½oz freshly grated Parmesan cheese

salt and freshly ground black pepper

Goat's cheese and mango

Feeds 6

Another Greens classic and probably one of the easiest dishes ever created, it's cheese on toast for goodness sake. This has been on and off the menu for thirteen years and there's still an argument raging as to who actually created it. The dish was conceived around a table at the Sangam curry house in Rusholme after a good few beers. Now we all claim to be the daddy of the dish, but I think we know the truth...

1 Preheat the oven to 120°C/250°F/mark 1/2. Dip a sharp knife into really hot water, then slice the cheese log into pieces about 8mm/⅓inch thick (this will give about six portions). Dip the knife into the water after each slice.

2 Combine the sesame seeds, chilli and mint in a wide bowl.

3 Warm the honey, then brush it sparingly on one side of each piece of cheese. Press the cheese slices into the sesame mixture then shake off any excess. Put to one side.

4 Cut a circle a little bigger than a cheese slice out of each piece of bread (probably a 7.5cm/3inch cutter). Brush each bread slice with a little oil, then put in the oven for about 5 minutes until dry, but not coloured.

5 To make the sauce, put the wine, mango and salt into a bowl and mix well.

6 When you're ready to serve, put a piece of cheese on each slice of bread and either put under a hot grill until the cheese softens, but not melts, or put it in a hottish oven (200°C/400°F/mark 6) for a few minutes.

7 Put a swirl or small pool of sauce in the middle of each plate, top with a little rocket, then sit the cheese on toast on top.

200g/7oz goat's cheese log, rind on
175g/6oz toasted sesame seeds
2 small red chillies, finely chopped
1 bunch of fresh mint leaves, finely chopped
5 tbsp clear honey
8 pieces thick sliced white loaf
olive oil
splash of white wine
200ml/7fl oz tinned mango pulp
pinch of salt
rocket leaves, to serve

Mushroom rarebit
on brioche toast

I love the taste and texture of field mushrooms and when you add the strong cheesy rarebit topping and serve it on toasted brioche, well, it's the food of kings and queens.

1 Preheat the oven to 180°C/350°F/mark 4. Put the mushrooms in a baking dish and season. Sprinkle with garlic and cover with the oil. Cook in the oven for 25 10–12 minutes until softened slightly.

2 Meanwhile, toast the brioche and make the rarebit by combining all the ingredients in a bowl. When the mushrooms come out of the oven spoon some of the rarebit mix onto each of them, pressing it well in. Then place under a hot grill until the cheese bubbles, melts and browns.

3 Serve one large mushroom on top of a piece of toasted brioche.

6 large field mushrooms, peeled and
trimmed
2 garlic cloves, crushed
100ml/3$\frac{1}{2}$fl oz olive oil
6 slices brioche
salt and freshly ground black pepper

For the rarebit

225g/8oz mature Cheddar or Gruyère
cheese, grated
1 tbsp wholegrain mustard
1 garlic clove, crushed
1 egg, beaten

Proper pizza

Pizzas originated in Naples as a way of using up leftovers, such as bread dough, tomatoes, cheese and herbs. Since then, of course, they've become a bit of a hybrid – asparagus and fontina, Sunday lunch pizza, even balti pizza. Well this is a simple, but delicious, Neapolitan pizza with tomatoes, cheese, basil and olive oil. Once you've mastered this, then if you want to try apricot and radish tikka masala pizza, well who am I to criticise?

1 To make the base, sift the flour into a large bowl. Dissolve the yeast in a little warm water until it begins to foam, then slowly add to the flour and mix to form a dough. If it's too sticky add more flour.

2 Cover the bowl and leave to rest for 5 minutes. Turn out onto a lightly floured surface and knead the dough with the salt for about 10 minutes until smooth. Cover with a damp cloth and let it prove for about 30 minutes.

3 Preheat the oven to 250ºC/475ºF/mark 9. Cut the dough in half, knead for a brief minute, then press it out into two circles about 4cm/1½inches diameter each (I like the edges slightly thicker, almost like a plate edge). Place the dough circles on floured baking trays.

4 To make the topping, season the tomatoes and spread over each dough base (you probably won't need the whole tin). Add some basil leaves, seasoning and torn cheese to each one, then drizzle over some oil.

5 Put in the oven and bake for 8–10 minutes.

6 Serve with a little more oil and some black pepper.

For the base

500g/1lb 2oz strong plain flour, plus extra for dusting

10g/¼oz fresh yeast

2 tsp salt

For the topping

400g tin of chopped tomatoes, well drained

fresh basil leaves

200g/7oz buffalo mozzarella cheese, torn

extra-virgin olive oil

salt and freshly ground black pepper

Pumpkin enchilladas with mole sauce

Feeds 6

I adore Mexican food – it can be a bit limited, but what's good is magnificent, like this dish. Mole sauce is a rich, deep, smoky sauce with both a chocolate and chilli hit. I leave the seeds in the chillies, but take them out if you prefer. I like to serve this with guacamole and soured cream. Don't turn the page thinking this weird choccy sauce isn't for you – it is! Try it and be converted.

1 To make the sauce, put the chillies, coriander seeds, sesame seeds, almonds, peppercorns and cloves in a mortar and pestle and crush. Tip into a frying pan and dry-fry for a minute or so until lightly charred.

2 In a separate pan, fry the onion, garlic and cocoa in a little oil for 2 minutes.

3 Add the tomatoes and bring to the boil, then add all the dry-fried spices, the cinnamon, sugar and stock and cook for 25 minutes. Transfer to a blender and whiz until smooth. Turn out and fold in the chocolate.

4 Preheat the oven to 200°C/400°F/mark 6. Put some oil in a roasting dish and put in the oven to heat up. Tip the squash into the roasting dish, season well and roast for 40 minutes until soft.

5 Put the squash in a bowl, add the refried beans, coriander and red chilli and stir to mix.

6 Divide the mixture between the tortillas, roll up and cut the ends straight. Put in a baking dish, cover, and cook in the oven for about 12 minutes, until warmed through.

7 To serve, put two tortillas on each plate and spoon over some of the sauce (it's pretty heady so not too much). Serve with some soured cream, lime wedges and coriander.

vegetable oil for roasting
2 butternut squash, peeled and
cut into 3cm/1¼inch cubes
400g tin of refried beans
freshly chopped coriander leaves
1 red chilli, chopped
12 soft flour or corn tortillas
salt and freshly ground black pepper
soured cream, lime wedges and
fresh coriander leaves, to serve

For the sauce

10 red chillies
2 tsp coriander seeds
1 tsp sesame seeds
25g/1oz flaked almonds
5 black peppercorns
2–3 cloves
1 onion, sliced
3 garlic cloves, crushed
1 tbsp cocoa powder
vegetable oil for frying
400g tin of chopped tomatoes
pinch of cinnamon
sugar to taste
150ml/5fl oz stock
100g/3½oz dark 70% cocoa-solids
chocolate, grated

Chinese mushroom pancakes

Feeds 6 as a starter, 3 as a main course

*Creating vegan dishes is always really difficult, so when I made this for the first time
I thought I was the vegan king! It takes its inspiration from crispy duck and pancakes,
but we're using oyster mushrooms instead – it really is brilliant.*

1 To make the sauce, heat a little oil in a frying pan and fry the shallots until soft.

2 Add the garlic and sherry, reduce a little, then add the plums and cook until
they begin to break down. Add the stock and bring to the boil.

3 Simmer for 5 minutes, then pass through a sieve into a serving bowl.

4 Mix the flour and five-spice powder together with some seasoning. Toss the
mushrooms in the mix, then shake off any excess.

5 Heat some oil in a large pan and deep-fry the mushrooms in batches for about
4 minutes, until crisp and brown. Drain well on kitchen paper.

6 Warm the pancakes either in a microwave for 20 seconds or in a steamer over
simmering water for 1 minute.

7 I like to pile the mushrooms onto one big plate, put the cucumber and spring
onions on another and the pancakes inside the steamer. Spread a little plum sauce
on a pancake, lay a strip of mushrooms down the middle, top with onion and
cucumber, and roll up, tucking in the bottom edge. Guzzle down and make sure
you've got extra pancakes on hand, because everyone will want more.

100g/3½oz plain flour

100g/3½oz five-spice powder

400g/14oz oyster mushrooms

18 Chinese pancakes, 7.5cm/3inch
diameter (from any Asian
supermarkets)

1 cucumber, deseeded and cut into
5cm/2inch batons

6–8 spring onions, finely sliced

vegetable oil for deep-frying

salt and freshly ground black pepper

For the plum sauce

2 shallots, chopped

1 garlic clove, crushed

splash of dry sherry

450g/1lb plums, stoned

100ml/3½fl oz stock

vegetable oil

Banana dhal

You can use any type of lentil to make a dhal, but the advantage of the red ones is that they don't have to be soaked, so this makes a really quick and easy meal. Adding either fresh banana or fried plantain makes it extra special and all you need to serve with it are a couple of chapattis.

1 Fry the onion, garlic and ginger in the oil over a low heat for about 10 minutes until soft and golden. Add the turmeric and cook for 1 minute.

2 Add the lentils to the pan and fry for 1–2 minutes.

3 Add the warmed stock and bring to the boil, then simmer for 15 minutes.

4 Add the spices, season and cook for a further 10 minutes.

5 A couple of minutes before serving fold in the bananas and warm through.

6 Garnish with coriander leaves and eat with bread.

1 onion, finely sliced

2 garlic cloves, chopped

2.5cm/1inch piece of fresh ginger, finely chopped

2 tbsp vegetable oil

pinch of turmeric

225g/8oz red lentils, well washed and drained

700ml/1¼ pints warmed stock

pinch of ground cumin

pinch of ground coriander

pinch of garam masala

4 firm bananas, thinly sliced

salt and freshly ground black pepper

fresh coriander leaves, to garnish

Gruyère-filled beef tomatoes

Feeds 4

This is a really old dish from Greens, but I still love it. The intense flavour from reducing the cream, then adding yummy Gruyère cheese and tasty treats makes it what I like to call a meat-eaters' veggie dish.

1 Preheat the oven to 170°C/325°F/mark 3. Skin the tomatoes by putting a cross on the bottom, plunging them into boiling water for about 30 seconds, then into iced water. The skins will peel off easily. Slice off the tops and put to one side, scoop out the pulp into a bowl, being careful not to break the flesh, and put the pulp to one side. Season the cavities well.

2 Put the cream in a heavy-based pan, bring slowly up to the boil, then cook to reduce the volume by half.

3 Meanwhile, heat a little oil in a large pan and gently fry the courgettes, peppers, mushrooms and garlic until soft, about 5 minutes.

4 Add 150g/5½oz of the cheese to the reduced cream and stir until it melts. Remove from the heat and fold in the fried vegetables.

5 Divide the filling between the tomatoes, top with the remaining cheese, sit the lids on top and put onto a baking tray.

6 Cook in the oven for 6–8 minutes, until the cheese melts.

7 To make the dressing, press the tomato pulp through a sieve and season the juices. Add the vinegar, then whisk in the oil.

8 Toss the rocket in the dressing and sit the tomatoes on top of the leaves.

4 beef tomatoes

400ml/14fl oz double cream

2 courgettes, finely diced

2 red peppers, deseeded and finely diced

75g/3oz white button mushrooms, finely chopped

1 garlic clove, crushed

200g/7oz freshly grated Gruyère cheese

vegetable oil for frying

salt and freshly ground black pepper

handful of fresh rocket leaves, to serve

For the dressing

tomato pulp from the tomatoes

1½ tbsp red wine vinegar

5 tbsp extra-virgin olive oil

Roasted red peppers with fennel

Feeds 6

Patience is the key for this recipe, the peppers and fennel need to be soft, and the cheese needs to brown and bubble – if you rush this it'll be a big disappointment.

1 Preheat the oven to 200°C/400°F/mark 6. Season the peppers well, drizzle with oil, then put in a baking tin and roast for about 10 minutes until softened.

2 Blanch the fennel pieces in boiling salted water for 2 minutes, then plunge into ice-cold water. When they're cool, pat dry.

3 Put the tomatoes and olives in a bowl with the garlic and parsley and season well.

4 Put a piece of fennel inside each pepper half, sprinkle some tomato mixture over and drizzle with oil. Top with grated cheese and put under a hot grill until the cheese bubbles and browns.

5 To serve, put a little watercress on each plate and sit a pepper half on top. Spoon some yoghurt on the side and garnish with a lemon wedge and green olives. Finish with a good twist of black pepper.

3 decent-sized red peppers, halved lengthways and deseeded

3 fennel bulbs, trimmed and cut into halves, or quarters if very large

3 tomatoes, skinned, deseeded and finely chopped

3–4 black olives, stoned and finely chopped

1 garlic clove, crushed

small handful of freshly chopped parsley

300g/10½oz mozzarella cheese, grated

olive oil for roasting

salt and freshly ground black pepper

watercress, Greek yoghurt, lemon wedges and green olives, to serve

Peas and carrots

Make this and don't tell your friends and family what's in it, they'll struggle to guess. Mint, peas, carrot vinaigrette – such simple ingredients, but combined they're pretty cool, and very much removed from the frozen or tinned stuff of school dinners. It makes a great starter.

1 Preheat the oven to 180°C/350°F/mark 4. Blanch the peas in boiling salted water for 1 minute, then plunge into ice-cold water. Drain well, then purée with the mint in a food processor.

2 Combine the eggs, cream and lemon juice in a bowl and season to taste. Pass the pea purée through a fine sieve into the egg mixture.

3 Divide the mixture between six greased ramekins. Put them in a bain-marie, cover with foil and cook in the oven for 25–30 minutes until set. Allow to cool.

4 To make the dressing, put 175ml/6fl oz of the carrot juice into a pan, bring to the boil, reduce the heat and cook until reduced by half. Pour into a bowl, add the honey and vinegar and whisk to mix. Slowly add the oil, then stir in the rest of the carrot juice and season.

5 Turn out each pea custard onto a plate. Toss some chard in the dressing, sit this on top of the pea creation and drizzle more dressing around.

350g/12oz fresh peas
lots of fresh mint leaves
3 eggs
175ml/6fl oz double cream
squeeze of lemon juice
salt and freshly ground black pepper
red chard, to garnish

For the dressing

225ml/8fl oz carrot juice (squeeze your own if you can)
1 tsp honey
1 tbsp white wine vinegar
150ml/5fl oz extra-virgin olive oil

Leeks wrapped
in filo

This is a simple and delicious starter packed with flavour. Avoid using really huge leeks as they're a bit 'woody' for this dish; what you need are slim, attractive leeks that will be sweet and succulent.

1 Preheat the oven to 220ºC/425ºF/mark 7. Cut the leeks into 10cm/4inch long pieces (cut the end at an angle to make them look pretty).

2 Heat some oil in a roasting tin, then put all the leeks in, season well and add the garlic. Roast in the oven for about 5 minutes until just a little soft. Take out of the oven and cool, then peel off their outer layer.

3 When the leeks are cool, cut the filo to the length of the leeks and wrap a piece around each leek. Brush with butter, put in the roasting tin and pop back in the oven for another 8–10 minutes until the filo is crisp and golden.

4 To make the dressing, whisk the lemon juice and mustard together, then add the garlic and whisk in the oil. Fold in the chives and tomatoes and season well.

5 Sit a little watercress on each plate, top with two leek parcels and spoon over a little dressing.

6 medium-sized leeks, trimmed, well washed and dried
1 garlic clove, sliced
6 sheets of filo pastry
75g/3oz melted butter
olive oil for roasting
salt and freshly ground black pepper
a little watercress, to serve

For the dressing

juice of 2 lemons
75g/3oz Dijon mustard
1 garlic clove, crushed
150ml/5fl oz extra-virgin olive oil
handful of freshly chopped chives
50g/2oz sun-blushed tomatoes, finely chopped

Leek and potato rosti with rarebit

Feeds 6

Rostis are simply fried grated potato with added bits – leeks in this case – and yummy toppings. They're easy to do: simply grate the spuds, mould into a disc and fry – but sometimes those pesky spuds don't want to stick together and you end up with burnt potato pieces, not nice. So this is a fail-safe way to perfect rosti every time, by par-boiling the spuds they'll stick like glue, and it means you can prepare them in advance without worrying about them.

1 Put the potatoes in a pan and just cover with water, bring to the boil and then boil for 7 minutes, no more. Drain.

2 When they're cool enough to handle, peel the potatoes and grate them into a bowl. If you use long strokes the end result is better, or you can use the grater attachment on your processor.

3 Mix the grated spuds with the leek and garlic, then season really well.

4 Mould the mixture into six patties and chill for 1 hour.

5 Heat a good amount of oil in a pan, enough so when you put the rosti in it will lap up the side a little. Pop in the rostis (do in two batches) and fry over a medium hot flame for about 4 minutes each side until golden, then drain on kitchen paper.

6 To make the topping, put the ingredients into a bowl and stir well to mix.

7 Lay out all the rostis on a baking sheet and divide the topping between them, then place under a hot grill until the cheese bubbles and browns.

8 This is delicious served with tomato and balsamic vinegar salad, or a fried egg – honestly!

4 large Maris Piper potatoes, or similar, scrubbed but unpeeled

1 small leek, trimmed, well washed and finely chopped

2 garlic cloves, crushed

vegetable oil for frying

lots of salt and freshly ground black pepper

For the topping

300g/10½oz freshly grated strong mature Cheddar cheese

1 egg, beaten

1½ tbsp wholegrain mustard

Beetroot tart

I love this and the combination of buttery pastry, sweet roasted beets and sharp tangy goat's cheese is delicious.

1 To make the pastry, put the butter, flour and salt in a food processor and pulse until it resembles breadcrumbs. Add the water and milk and pulse to form a dough. Turn into a bowl, cover and chill for 25 minutes.

2 Preheat the oven to 200°C/400°F/mark 6. Divide the pastry into four and roll out to roughly fit deep tart cases, about 10–12.5cm/4–4½inches wide. Line the cases, letting the pastry overhang the edges a little, and bake blind for 25–30 minutes until firm and lightly golden. Remove from the oven and trim off the edges.

3 To make the chutney, fry the onions, garlic and butter with some seasoning in a little oil over a low heat for about 20 minutes until golden but not burnt. Add the sugar and vinegar, bring to the boil, then reduce the heat right the way down and cook for about 30 minutes until 'jammy'.

4 To make the filling, chuck the broccoli into boiling salted water, count to 10, then spoon it out and plunge into iced water (this will stop it cooking on). Drain well.

5 Heat some oil in a frying pan, then add the beetroots, season well and cook for a couple of minutes. Add the broccoli and pine nuts (these are yummy if you toast them a little first) and cook for a minute or two. Pour in the passata and toss all the ingredients quickly, then remove from the heat.

6 Divide the filling mixture between the cases and top with the crumbled goat's cheese. Either flash under a hot grill until the cheese browns, or put back into the top of the oven for a few minutes.

7 Serve alongside the chutney. This is really fab with big fat square chips with rock salt and balsamic vinegar.

For the pastry

200g/7oz chilled butter, cut into cubes

400g/14oz plain flour

pinch of salt

50ml/2fl oz water

50ml/2fl oz milk

For the filling

12 broccoli florets

4–6 cooked beetroots, peeled and cut into large wedges

75g/3oz pine nuts

100ml/3½fl oz passata

150g/5½oz goat's cheese, crumbled

vegetable oil for frying

salt and freshly ground black pepper

For the chutney

4 large Spanish onions, sliced

1 garlic clove, crushed

50g/2oz butter

100g/3½oz dark brown sugar

125ml/4fl oz white wine vinegar

vegetable oil for frying

salt and freshly ground black pepper

Simple
tomato tart

Feeds 4

Every time I make this I forget how easy it is and yet it looks like you've taken ages to make it. Serve with some rocket dressed with extra-virgin olive oil and balsamic vinegar.

1 Preheat the oven to 180°C/350°F/mark 4. Roll out the pastry on a lightly floured surface to an 18 x 28cm/7 x 11inch rectangle and put on a greased baking tray.

2 Cut the tomatoes into slices as thick as a pound coin. Arrange overlapping slices on the pastry, leaving a 2.5cm/1inch border all round. Season well, brush with butter and sprinkle with sugar.

3 Bake in the oven for 25–30 minutes, until crisp and golden and the tomatoes have caramelised.

4 Combine the oil and vinegar in a bowl and toss the rocket in it. Serve a generous slice of tart on each plate with the dressed rocket.

225g/8oz bought puff pastry

flour for dusting

6–8 plum tomatoes, peeled

2 tbsp melted butter, plus extra for greasing

1 tbsp caster sugar

3 tbsp extra-virgin olive oil

1 tbsp balsamic vinegar

fresh rocket leaves

salt and freshly ground black pepper

Sun-dried tomato, mozzarella and basil tart

Feeds 6

This is so simple and yet so tasty. If you ever make a cheese-filled tart, always add a little splash of cream to give a touch of richness to the filling. All you need with this is a bit of green salad dressed with simple vinaigrette.

1 Divide the pastry into six equal pieces and roll out on a lightly floured surface to fit six 10cm/4inch tart cases. Press the pastry into the cases, then chill them for about 20 minutes.

2 Preheat the oven to 200°C/400°F/mark 6. Put the cases on a baking tray and bake for 15 minutes until crisp and golden.

3 To make the filling, combine the cheese, basil and tomatoes in a large bowl and season well.

4 When the cases are cooked, remove from the oven, divide the filling between the cases and add a splash of cream to each. Return to the oven and bake for about 5 minutes until the cheese melts and begins to brown.

1 quantity of shortcrust pastry (see page 92)

flour for dusting

300g/10½oz freshly grated mozzarella cheese

about 20 fresh basil leaves

12 sun-dried tomatoes, finely chopped

dash of double cream

salt and freshly ground black pepper

Spicy beetroot and coconut soup

Feeds 6

Beetroot gets a lot of bad press and everybody, except me, seems to hate pickled beetroot. I love it and it also has magical properties. Whenever I go to watch an important Liverpool football match with my mates, it's tradition for me to bring the lucky cheese and beetroot sandwiches – they nearly always work. Anyway, this is one of the most stunning and delicious soups you'll ever make, it's both earthy and spicy at the same time and it has the best colour pink. A little tip: don't blend it until you're about to serve as it will go brownish.

1 Put all the ingredients for the paste into a blender and blend until smooth (the smoother the paste the nicer the soup, so take your time).

2 Preheat the oven to 200ºC/ 400ºF/mark 6. Put the scrubbed beets into an ovenproof dish, sprinkle with oil and sea salt, then wrap in foil and roast for about 35 minutes until soft. When cool enough to handle, peel and chop the beets.

3 Gently fry the shallots and cumin seeds in a little oil, then add half the paste and cook for 5 minutes to release the fragrance.

4 Add half the beets, cook for a couple of minutes, then add the stock, bring to the boil and simmer for about 7–8 minutes.

5 This is when it gets interesting – just before serving, put the soup, coconut milk, the rest of the paste and beetroot in a blender and blend until smooth. It will be a bright pink, like you've never seen from food before, unless you live on Mars. The soup should be hot enough, but if necesssary reheat gently for a minute or two.

6 Check the seasoning, then serve immediately topped with mint, coriander and cucumber. It's also lovely with the coriander seed flat bread (see page 12).

500g/1lb 2oz fresh beetroot, scrubbed

vegetable oil for coating and frying

2 banana shallots, finely chopped

1 tsp cumin seeds

600ml/1 pint stock

400ml tin of coconut milk

sea salt

fresh mint, coriander leaves and chopped, deseeded cucumber, to serve

For the paste

2 stalks of lemon grass

2 garlic cloves

3 red chillies (deseeded if you like)

5cm/1inch piece of fresh ginger, peeled

4 kaffir lime leaves

juice of 1 lime

Big platefuls

Huevos rancheros (ranch eggs)

Feeds 4

A good few years ago my dear friend Graham Peers got married in Richmond, Virginia, USA, so a tribe of us made the trip over and we all stayed at various friends of Graham's around town. Alison, my wife, and I got the best deal as we were 50 yards from a fantastic place called The Steak and Eggs Kitchen, which did the best breakfasts, and had those mini-tellies on the tables. Well, this is where I first had huevos rancheros, or fried eggs cooked with spicy salsa and flour tortillas on the side. Serve these with extra-hot chilli sauce and endless cups of 'cwarfee'.

1 Put all the ingredients for the salsa except the passata in a bowl and season. Gradually add the passata – you may find you don't need it all, you're looking for the veg bits to be bound by the tomato sauce, not swimming in it.

2 You need to cook this in batches. Heat a little oil in a frying pan over a medium heat and warm a quarter of the salsa. Now make a hole in the middle of the pan, melt 50g/2oz of the butter in the gap, then break 2 eggs into this space. Put a lid on the pan and leave for about 3 minutes. The dish is ready when the eggs are cooked and the whites have merged into the salsa.

3 Slide the eggs and salsa onto a large plate and top with coriander leaves. Cook the rest of the eggs in the same way. Now dip your warm tortillas into the yolks and dare yourself to overdo the chilli sauce. (Not that I'd know, but apparently this is a great hangover cure!)

vegetable oil for frying

225g/8oz butter

8 eggs

fresh coriander leaves

2 warm soft flour or corn tortillas, halved

hot chilli sauce (Jamaican hot is pretty good)

For the salsa

1 onion, finely chopped

1 red pepper, deseeded and finely chopped

1 small bird's eye chilli, finely chopped

1 courgette, finely chopped

1 garlic clove, finely chopped

1 green pepper, deseeded and finely chopped

150ml/5fl oz passata

salt and freshly ground black pepper

Savoury Paris-Brest

Feeds 6–8

This is traditionally a sweet dish with custard, almonds and other yummy things inside a ring of choux pastry. I don't see any reason why you can't turn it on its head and have a savoury filling – so I will.

1 Preheat the oven to 200°C/400°F/mark 6. To make the pastry, put the butter and water in a pan and heat until the butter melts, then bring to the boil. Take the pan off the heat, tip in all the flour and mix well. Cool slightly, then, using a wooden spoon, beat in the eggs, one at a time (it's pretty tough on the old arms, this one). Add the salt.

2 Transfer to a piping bag and allow to cool for a few minutes. Line a baking tray with greaseproof paper, then pipe a 20cm/8inch diameter circle onto the paper, then pipe another one directly on top.

3 Put the tray in the oven and cook for 30–40 minutes, when the choux ring should be golden and firm. The aim is to get it to dry out in the middle – I quite often put it on the bottom shelf for another 5–10 minutes to make sure. When it's cooked, take the ring out and let it cool. Increase the oven temperature to 220°C/425°F/mark 7.

4 To make the filling, heat some oil on a baking tray in the oven. Slice the courgettes and aubergine into pieces as thick as a pound coin. Ideally, cook each vegetable separately – season each vegetable, place in the hot oil on the tray, add a little garlic and roast until soft, then toss in a little thyme. Put to one side while you cook the next one. However, if you're pushed for time, roast the onions for 5 minutes, then add the peppers for 5 minutes, then the aubergine and courgettes in the same tray.

5 When all the vegetables are roasted, reduce the oven temperature to 180°C/350°F/mark 4. Slice the choux ring horizontally into two halves. Arrange the vegetables on the bottom ring and top with the sun-blushed tomatoes and goat's cheese. Cover with the top ring.

6 Pop it back into the oven for about 10 minutes until the cheese softens. Serve with a dressed mixed leaf salad.

150g/5½ oz butter
225ml/8fl oz water
225g/8oz plain flour
6 eggs
pinch of salt

For the filling

2 courgettes
1 aubergine
1 red onion, sliced in quarters attached to the base
2 red peppers, deseeded and cut into chunks
1 garlic clove
fresh thyme
12 sun-blushed tomatoes
200g/7oz goat's cheese, crumbled
vegetable oil for roasting
salt and freshly ground black pepper

Filo strudel with port wine sauce

Feeds 6

OK, here we go, the recipe that changed the world, well Greens. I always say this is the dish to serve to meat-eaters because it blows their minds. I like to serve it with some fine beans with garlic and tomato sauce (see page 106) and a few new potatoes, although a good friend of mine swears it tastes best with chips and garlic mayo. If you make only one dish out of this book, it should be this one...

1 Heat some oil in a pan, add the mushrooms, garlic and seasoning and fry for a couple of minutes, then drain well. Then fry the leeks.

2 Mix the cheeses together in a large bowl with a good amount of seasoning until smooth. (Sometimes it helps to warm the cream cheese for a few seconds in a microwave to soften it.) Fold in the mushrooms, leeks and tomatoes, then chill for at least 2 hours.

3 Preheat the oven to 200°C/400°F/mark 6. Lay out six pieces of pastry on a lightly floured surface and brush with lots of melted butter, then cover with another layer and brush again. Add a final layer, but this time only brush the edges of the pastry.

4 Divide the chilled filling into six long sausages and place each one on the bottom edge of each pastry rectangle. Fold the bottom edge over the filling, tuck in the sides, then roll up into a tight parcel and brush with butter. Put them all on a baking tray and cook in the oven for 25 minutes until crisp and golden.

5 Meanwhile, make the sauce. Pour the wine into a pan, bring to the boil and reduce it by half – stick a bay leaf in the wine if you want to make it a little more 'herby'.

6 Heat the oil in a pan and cook the onion, mushrooms and garlic with seasoning until soft. Throw in a big slosh of port and reduce that by half. Next, pour in the reduced wine and bring back to the boil, then add the stock, bring to the boil and cook to reduce for about 15 minutes. Just before serving, whisk in the cold butter to give it a really great shine, or cook down further to make more of a chutney.

7 To serve, pour a little sauce on each plate and sit a strudel on top.

200g/7oz button mushrooms, halved

1 garlic clove, crushed

200g/7oz leeks, trimmed, well washed, drained and roughly chopped

250g/9oz ricotta cheese

250g/9oz full-fat cream cheese

3 tomatoes, skinned, deseeded and chopped

18 pieces filo pastry, 23 x 15cm/ 9 x 6inch

melted butter

olive oil for frying

salt and freshly ground black pepper

For the sauce

1 bottle red wine (a good heavy red is best)

1 bay leaf (optional)

2 tbsp olive oil

1 large onion, sliced

75g/3oz button mushrooms, sliced

2 garlic cloves, crushed

good glug of port

100ml/3½fl oz stock

25g/1oz cold butter, cubed

Wild mushroom pancakes

Feeds 6

The filling for these pancakes is rich and delicious and the pecans make it a brilliant dish for the winter. Unlike in most pancake recipes, you don't need to let the batter stand.

1 First make the pancakes. Sift the flour and salt into a bowl, then make a well in the centre and break the eggs into it. Whisk the eggs into the flour, then, little by little, slowly add the milk and water, whisking well to avoid lumps. Finally, whisk in the butter.

2 Heat a little oil in an 18cm/7inch frying pan until really hot, then turn the heat down to medium. Spoon about 4 tbsp of batter into the pan and swirl it around to evenly coat the base. Cook the pancake for about 30 seconds, then flip it over and cook the other side. Turn the pancake out onto greaseproof paper and repeat with the rest of the batter. You should get twelve pancakes. Stack each pancake on greaseproof paper until you're ready to use them.

3 For the filling, mix the ricotta and Parmesan cheeses together and season well.

4 Heat a little oil in a pan and fry the fresh shiitakes and garlic for about 5 minutes, then drain on kitchen paper. Drain off the water from the dried mushrooms and chop them up.

5 Combine all the mushrooms, the pecans and tarragon with the cheese mixture and check the seasoning.

6 Preheat the oven to 180°C/350°F/mark 4. Put about 4 tbsp of filling across each pancake and roll up, tucking in the ends to make a neat parcel.

7 Use two pancakes per serving. Put the pancakes on a greased baking tray or in pairs in greased individual dishes and top each pair with grated mozzarella. Cook in the oven for about 15 minutes until the cheese melts. Serve with a little ladleful of warm tomato sauce and some fine beans with garlic and tomato sauce (see page 106).

100g/3½oz plain flour

pinch of salt

2 eggs

200ml/7fl oz milk

75ml/3fl oz water

50g/2oz butter, melted

200g/7oz freshly grated mozzarella cheese

vegetable oil for frying

½ quantity basic tomato sauce (see page 107), to serve

For the filling

450g/1lb ricotta cheese

150g/5½oz freshly grated Parmesan cheese

175g/6oz fresh shiitake mushrooms

1 garlic clove, crushed

75g/3oz dried shiitake mushrooms, soaked in boiling water for 1 hour

100g/3½oz slightly broken pecans

50g/2oz freshly chopped tarragon leaves

salt and freshly ground black pepper

Hazelnut and mushroom parcels

Feeds 4

This is another 'meaty' dish that any carnivores will adore. Mushrooms, hazelnuts and cheese wrapped in puff pastry – how could that not be anything but gorgeous? Great for Sunday lunch, or even Christmas, maybe with some fresh cranberries inside and a Cumberland sauce, but equally delicious for your tea tonight.

1 To make the parcels, fry the shallots and garlic in a little oil until soft, then add the chestnut mushrooms and cook until soft. Add the assorted mushrooms, nuts and port and reduce a little. Finally, add the butter, cook for 2 minutes, then remove from the heat and drain for at least 1 hour, or as long as possible.

2 Put a piece of vignotte on each piece of pastry, then top with some of the mushroom mixture. Roll up into a parcel and put on a greased baking tray. Brush with eggwash, top with sesame seeds and chill for at least 20 minutes.

3 Preheat the oven to 200°C/400°F/mark 6. Cook the parcels for 20 minutes until the pastry is golden.

4 Meanwhile, make the sauce. Heat some oil in a large pan and fry the shallots and garlic for 5 minutes until softened. Add the wine and reduce by half.

5 Chuck in the red peppers and cook for 5 minutes, then add the stock and tarragon and bring to the boil. Cook for 5 minutes, then pour into a food processor and whiz until smooth. Turn out into a dish, season and add a splash of vinegar to cut the sweet sauce.

6 Spoon a little sauce onto each plate, and top with a parcel. Garnish with watercress.

2 shallots

1 garlic clove, crushed

200g/7oz chestnut mushrooms, cut into bite-sized chunks

250g/9oz assorted mushrooms, cut into bite-sized chunks

100g/3½oz shelled, roasted hazelnuts

splash of port

small piece of cold butter, plus extra for greasing

200g/7oz vignotte cheese

4 x 15cm/6inch square pieces puff pastry rolled out to 2–3mm/ ½inch thick

1 egg, beaten, for eggwash

handful of sesame seeds

olive oil for frying

a little watercress, to garnish

For the sauce

2 shallots

1 garlic clove

splash of white wine

6 red peppers, roasted, skinned, deseeded and chopped

200ml/7fl oz stock

sprig of fresh tarragon

splash of white wine vinegar

Sweet potato and
pineapple sandwich

Feeds 4

I love sweet potato, it has such a silky smooth texture when it's mashed and a delicious caramel flavour when it's roasted. This dish gets its inspiration from the Caribbean, where there are so many delicious sweet yet savoury recipes that it's impossible to be anything other than a complete pig when you visit. You can give this an even bigger Caribbean flavour by adding a slug of rum to the pan when stir-frying the veggies.

1 Preheat the oven to 220ºC/425ºF/mark 7. Heat the oil in a roasting tin, then add the sweet potato chunks. Season well, give them a good shake and add the chillies, thyme and garlic. Roast for about 30 minutes until the sweet potato is soft (it's probably worth giving them the odd stir while they're roasting).

2 Brush each of the pineapple slices with oil and cook on a hot griddle pan for a couple of minutes each side until well striped. When they've all been charred, put them in an ovenproof dish with their juice and put to one side.

3 To make the sauce, cook the curry paste in a saucepan for a few minutes to release the flavour, then add the coconut milk and bring to the boil. Add the stock and cook for 5 minutes.

4 Heat some more oil in a frying pan, add the onion and cook until it starts to brown. Add the red pepper and then the sweet potatoes. Cook for 3–4 minutes until the potato starts to break down.

5 Spoon in a little of the curry sauce to bind the mixture, then add the okra and coriander. Stir it around for another couple of minutes.

6 Pop the pineapple slices in the oven for a few minutes to warm through. Put a slice of pineapple on each plate, then spoon a quarter of the sweet potato mixture on top (if you've got them, use small rings to make it neater). Sit another slice of pineapple on top and drizzle some of the curry sauce around the edge.

100ml/3½fl oz vegetable oil
600g/1lb 5oz golden sweet potatoes, peeled and cut into largish bite-sized chunks
2 small red chillies, chopped
handful of fresh thyme
4 garlic cloves, crushed
1 pineapple, peeled and cut into 8 slices (keep the juice)
1 red onion, sliced
1 red pepper, deseeded and sliced
75g/3oz blanched okra
freshly chopped coriander leaves
salt and freshly ground black pepper

For the curry sauce

3 tbsp curry paste (mild or hot, whatever's in the cupboard)
400ml tin of coconut milk
100ml/3½fl oz stock

Lancashire cheese sausages with onion gravy

Makes about 12 sausages

The joy of a good sausage is that fried, fatty quality and a strong mystery seasoning. Veggie sausages are tricky, but after years of trying I think this is a pretty good version – when you break them open they look 'fatty' and they taste like a dream.

1 The sausage mix couldn't be easier – just chuck all the ingredients except the oil into a large bowl, season well, get your hands in and mix it all up. When you taste it, I reckon you need to over-season it by about 15 per cent, so it's a bit more salty and peppery than you'd normally have – the mixture seems to lose some of its power as it chills and cooks. Chill the mixture for 2 hours.

2 Meanwhile, make the gravy. Heat a little oil in a pan and fry the onions, garlic and sugar over a low heat until golden. Sprinkle on the flour and cook for 3–4 minutes. Add the gravy browning and stock and bring to the boil. Season, then simmer for at least 20 minutes.

3 Mould the chilled sausage mix into sausage shapes – you should get about twelve decent bangers out of it, depending how big you like your sausage... You can either shallow-fry the sausages in a little oil or deep-fry them in a lot of oil; I think the deep-fry method brings the best out of the flavour and texture. Fry them for about 5 minutes until golden, then drain well on some kitchen paper and serve with the gravy.

4 This fabulous grub is great with mashed potato (try it with the addition of wholegrain mustard), with a salad or in a bun smothered in ketchup, onions and mustard and served with chips.

For the sausages

600g/1lb 5oz Lancashire cheese, grated or crumbled

200g/7oz fresh breadcrumbs

6 spring onions, chopped

2 tbsp fresh thyme, chopped

2 tbsp freshly chopped parsley

3 whole eggs, plus 3 egg yolks

2 garlic cloves, crushed

about 50ml/2fl oz milk, to bind

salt and freshly ground black pepper

vegetable oil for frying

For the onion gravy

3 large onions, sliced

2 garlic cloves, crushed

1 tbsp brown sugar

75g/3oz plain flour

75ml/3fl oz gravy browning

500ml/18fl oz stock

Penne all'arabiata

Feeds 4

This is one of the simplest pasta dishes in the world and definitely one of the most delicious. It's particularly good if you grow your own tomatoes as their sweet earthiness makes it even better.

1 Cook the pasta in boiling salted water until al dente. Meanwhile, heat the oil in a pan and gently fry the shallots, chillies and garlic until soft, then add the tomatoes and turn up the heat. Once the tomatoes begin to break up, turn down the heat and simmer for about 5 minutes to form a sauce.

2 Drain the pasta over a saucepan and add to the sauce with a little of the water the pasta was cooked in. Season well and stir in the parsley. Serve with big shavings of Parmesan, crusty bread and a fruity Valpolicella red wine.

300g/10½oz dried penne

100ml/3½fl oz olive oil

2 shallots, finely chopped

2 small red bird's eye chillies, deseeded and chopped

1 garlic clove, crushed

8 tomatoes, finely chopped

a good handful of freshly chopped parsley

salt and freshly ground black pepper

Parmesan shavings, to serve

Macaroni
cheese

Feeds 4

Real comfort food – a bowl of creamy macaroni cheese never fails to hit the spot. In this recipe I've added both cherry and sun-blushed tomatoes to make it more of a sunshine dish. If you pack the mac-cheese into a presentation ring before it goes into the oven you can make it poncy enough for an informal lunch/dinner for friends. But if you're doing it for yourself, slap it into a big bowl and wade in.

1 Preheat the oven to 200ºC/400ºF/mark 6. To make the sauce, pour the milk into a pan, add the bay leaves and heat to scalding point. Remove from the heat and, when cooled a little, discard the bay leaves.

2 Melt the butter in a pan, stir in the flour and cook, stirring, for 3 minutes (don't let it brown). Add a little of the milk to the flour and stir to combine. Cook briefly, then gradually add the rest of the milk and stir until you have a smooth sauce. Bring to the boil, stirring all the time, reduce the heat and simmer for 3 minutes. Take off the heat and stir in the cheese, mustard and seasoning.

3 Heat the oil in a large pan and fry the shallots until translucent, then add the pasta, all the tomatoes and the cheese sauce. The sauce should coat, not swamp, the macaroni (you may need to add a little milk to loosen the sauce).

4 Heat through, then pour into an ovenproof dish and sprinkle with Parmesan. Bake in the oven for 6–8 minutes until the sauce begins to thicken.

5 Finish off under a hot grill, and top with chopped parsley.

2 tbsp olive oil

4 shallots, sliced

400g/14oz cooked macaroni

20 cherry tomatoes, halved

12 sun-blushed tomatoes

freshly grated Parmesan cheese

freshly chopped parsley

For the cheese sauce

500ml/18fl oz pints milk

2 bay leaves

25g/1oz butter

25g/1oz plain flour

150g/5½oz mature Cheddar or Gruyère cheese, grated

1 tsp English mustard

salt and freshly ground black pepper

Linguine with potato and pesto

Feeds 4

More comfort food – potato and pasta is a great combination, if you don't feel like it's a carb overload. Add strong pesto and creamy mascarpone and you may never leave the house again.

1 To make the pesto, put all the ingredients except the oil into a blender and blend until smooth. Then, with the motor running, slowly add enough oil to make a thick sauce.

2 Cook the pasta in loads of boiling salted water for about 8 minutes.

3 Very finely dice the spuds and put in water. Heat the oil in a frying pan. Drain and dry the spuds and fry, stirring continuously, until crisp and golden. Don't allow them to burn. Take them off the heat and drain on kitchen paper.

4 Drain the cooked pasta, then put it back in the saucepan. Add all the remaining ingredients and the pesto to the pasta and warm through. Check the seasoning.

5 Serve with black pepper and Parmesan shavings – this is delicious.

400g/14oz dried linguine

2 Maris Piper spuds, peeled

50ml/2fl oz olive oil

2 garlic cloves, crushed

200g/7oz mascarpone cheese

100ml/3½fl oz stock

salt and freshly ground black pepper

Parmesan shavings, to serve

For the pesto

200g/7oz pine nuts

large bunch of fresh basil leaves

150g/5½oz freshly grated Parmesan cheese

2 garlic cloves

extra-virgin olive oil

Gnocchi with wild mushroom and rosemary ragu

Once you've made this dish it will become a firm favourite in your repertoire. It's packed full of flavour, taste and texture and the smell when you're cooking it is heaven. I reckon this'll feed about 12 of you, but I find if you reduce the quantities it doesn't work as well, so invite all those people round you haven't seen for absolutely ages.

1 To make the gnocchi, boil the spuds for about 40 minutes until soft. Drain, and when cool enough to handle peel and mash or pass through a ricer into a bowl.

2 Make a well in the centre of the mash, add the egg and mix in, then add the flour and seasoning. Mix to form a dough, then knead for a few minutes until dry to the touch.

3 Divide the potato dough into three and roll each out into 2cm/¾inch diameter ropes, then cut off at 2cm/¾inch intervals. Press one side of each gnocchi with the back of a fork to form 'grooves' – this will give the sauce something to stick to.

4 Bring a large pan of water to the boil and drop the gnocchi into the water. When they rise to the top, scoop out and refresh in ice-cold water. Drain well, then pat dry, toss in oil and chill until needed. You can also freeze them at this stage.

5 To make the ragu, heat some oil in a pan and gently fry the vegetables for 5 minutes until soft. Add the tomato paste and cook for 7–8 minutes until a rich red.

6 Add the wine, stock and rosemary, bring to the boil, then simmer for at least 40 minutes, but preferably 1 hour.

7 When ready to serve, cut the mushrooms into chunks and fry with the garlic in oil until soft, season well.

8 Warm the gnocchi in the ragu, spoon onto a plate and top with the mushrooms and Parmesan.

600g/1lb 5oz floury potato, e.g. Russet, unpeeled
1 large egg
450g/1lb plain flour
salt and freshly ground black pepper

For the ragu

olive oil for frying and tossing
2 onions, finely chopped
2 carrots, finely chopped
2 celery stalks, finely chopped
2 garlic cloves, crushed
300g/10½oz tomato paste
850ml/1½ pints red wine
850ml/1½ pints stock
fresh rosemary to taste

For the topping

450g/1lb Portobello mushrooms
1 garlic clove
freshly grated Parmesan cheese, to serve

Goat's cheese cannelloni with cherry tomatoes

Feeds 6

I got a bit fed up with cannelloni baked in either tomato or béchamel sauce, so I started roasting little cherry tomatoes in lots of oil, to make a semi-sauce. This is packed full of flavour and looks divine.

1 Preheat the oven to 220°C/425°F/mark 7. Pour some oil into a roasting tin and put in the oven to heat up. Chuck the tomatoes into the hot tin and roast for about 10 minutes.

2 Add the thyme, balsamic vinegar, garlic and seasoning and roast for a further 15 minutes, then remove the tin from the oven and keep warm. Reduce the oven temperature to 180°C/350°F/mark 4.

3 Make the filling by combining the cheeses and spinach with lots of seasoning in a bowl.

4 Lay the pasta out and put a line of filling along the long edge of each piece, then roll up into a cannelloni shape.

5 Drizzle a little of the oil from the tomatoes on the bottom of an ovenproof dish large enough to hold all 12 cannelloni. Then pack the tubes in and pour the tomatoes over. Bake in the oven for 15 minutes until heated through.

6 Serve topped with shaved Parmesan and a crisp green salad dressed with oil and balsamic vinegar.

400g/14oz cherry tomatoes, halved
fresh thyme
dash of balsamic vinegar
2 garlic cloves, crushed
12 sheets of fresh pasta, 12.5 x 10cm/4½ x 4inches square
olive oil for roasting
salt and freshly ground black pepper
Parmesan shavings, to serve

For the filling

200g/7oz ricotta cheese
150g/5½oz goat's cheese
150g/5½oz freshly grated Parmesan cheese
100g/3½oz baby spinach leaves, well washed and drained

Lemon grass risotto
with lime leaf tapenade

Feeds 4 for lunch

As long as you add warm stock to the rice, don't stir it too much and let it know you love it, making risotto is very straightforward. This fragrant variation is delicious – the lemon grass is so uplifting.

1 Fry the shallots and garlic in a little oil until soft. Bruise the lemon grass with the back of a knife and add to the pan. Add the rice and stir gently for a couple of minutes until the edge of the rice becomes translucent. Then add the wine and cook for a minute or two.

2 Add a good ladleful of stock to the rice and cook, stirring, until it has been absorbed. Repeat with more stock until it has all been used and/or the rice is soft. Season well.

3 To make the tapenade, simply put all the ingredients except the oil in a food processor, add seasoning and blend. When it's pretty broken down, leave the motor running and slowly add the oil. Spoon out into a bowl.

4 Add a swirl of cream to the rice just before serving, then divide between four bowls and top each serving with some tapenade.

4 shallots, sliced

1 garlic clove, crushed

3 stalks of lemon grass

450g/1lb arborio rice

splash of white wine

650ml/22fl oz stock

splash of cream

vegetable oil for frying

salt and freshly ground black pepper

For the tapenade

8 fresh kaffir lime leaves, torn

100g/3½oz green olives, stoned

1 tbsp capers

handful of coriander stalks

1 garlic clove

juice and zest of 1 lime

75ml/3fl oz olive oil

Moroccan spaghetti

Feeds 4

One of the best places I've been to is Marrakesh – the sights, sounds, smells and people are so stimulating. The food market at Djemma el-Fna square has some of the best street food anywhere, with its wonderful aromas of cinnamon, almonds and cumin. So this is inspired by that trip; it's simple pasta with a sauce a-la-Marrakesh.

1 Cook the spaghetti in boiling salted water until al dente.

2 Meanwhile, heat the oil in a pan and gently fry the onion and garlic until soft.

3 Add the tomatoes, cinnamon, cumin and turmeric and cook over a medium heat for about 20 minutes until the tomatoes break down.

4 Season the sauce and then add the almonds and chick peas.

5 Drain the pasta and divide between four plates. Fold the herbs into the sauce and mix it with the pasta.

300g/10½oz dried spaghetti

100ml/3½fl oz olive oil

1 onion, finely chopped

2 garlic cloves, crushed

8 tomatoes, finely chopped

1 tsp ground cinnamon

1 tsp ground cumin

pinch of turmeric

100g/3½oz toasted, flaked almonds

100g/3½oz cooked chick peas, drained and rinsed if tinned

bunch each of fresh parsley and coriander leaves, finely chopped

handful of freshly chopped mint leaves

salt and freshly ground black pepper

Four-cheese and courgette penne

Feeds 4

An easy pasta dish that shows how essential it is to use good ingredients in simple dishes. I like to cook the courgettes slowly so they almost begin to 'melt'. Watch out for the salt – you don't need much at all as the cheeses will provide it.

1 Cook the penne in lots of boiling salted water until al dente.

2 While it is cooking, fry the courgettes and garlic slowly in some oil until very soft. Season to taste.

3 Put all the cheeses in a separate pan with a little splash of oil and slowly warm through until they begin to melt. Add a splash of wine and the courgettes and cook very gently for 4–5 minutes.

4 Drain the pasta over a saucepan, then add the pasta to the courgette mixture, together with a little of its cooking water.

5 Stir to mix, check the seasoning and turn out into a serving dish. Top with some Parmesan shavings and serve at once.

400g/14oz dried penne

450g/1lb courgettes, washed and cut into discs

1 garlic clove, chopped

100g/3½oz mascarpone cheese

100g/3½oz freshly grated Parmesan cheese

100g/3½oz Gorgonzola cheese

100g/3½oz Dolcelatte cheese

splash of white wine

olive oil for frying

salt and freshly ground black pepper

Parmesan shavings, to serve

Aubergine tikka masala

Feeds 6

Apparently, chicken tikka masala is now the UK's favourite dish, more than roast dinner and more than fish and chips. If that's the case, then I feel it's only right and proper for there to be a vegetarian version.

1 Toss the aubergines in vegetable oil and salt. Cook on a hot griddle pan until striped on each side.

2 Combine all the marinade ingredients in a bowl, season with salt and coat the aubergine pieces well. Thread onto wooden skewers, put in a tray, cover and chill for at least 2 hours.

3 Meanwhile, make the sauce. Put the onion, garlic and chillies in a food processor and blend until smooth. Heat the peanut oil in a pan and fry the onion paste over a low heat for about 7 minutes until golden brown.

4 Roughly chop the coriander leaves and put with the ginger and tomatoes in the processor (don't bother washing it out) and blend until smooth.

5 Once the onions are golden, spoon the tomato mixture into the pan and cook for a good 15 minutes, until most of the liquid has evaporated.

6 Stir in the ground coriander, cumin, paprika, fenugreek and garam masala and add salt to taste. Cook briefly, then gently stir in the yoghurt, a little at a time, to avoid curdling.

7 Add the milk, crank the heat right up and bring to the boil. Simmer for 5 minutes.

8 Cook the aubergine skewers under a hot grill, basting with the butter and lemon juice and turning when golden. (They are delicious eaten just like this with a naan bread wrapped around them.)

9 Lay 2 skewers of aubergine tikka on a plate, spoon over some sauce and garnish with coriander leaves. Serve with rice, naan bread and icy cold lager.

4–6 aubergines (about 900g/2lb in weight), cut into chunks or wedges
vegetable oil
50ml/2fl oz melted butter
juice of 1 lemon
salt
fresh coriander leaves, to garnish

For the marinade

100ml/3½fl oz natural yoghurt
juice of 1 lime
2 garlic cloves, crushed
2.5cm/1inch piece of fresh ginger, finely chopped
1 tbsp ground coriander
1 tsp each of ground cumin, garam masala, paprika

For the sauce

1 onion, roughly chopped
5 garlic cloves
3–5 red chillies (deseeded if you like)
3 tbsp peanut oil
1 bunch of fresh coriander leaves
4cm/1½inch piece of fresh ginger
5 plum tomatoes
1 tbsp ground coriander, 2 tsp ground cumin, 1 tsp paprika, 2 tsp ground fenugreek, 1 tsp garam masala
50ml/2fl oz natural yoghurt
150ml/5fl oz milk

Rendang shallot and asparagus curry

Feeds 6

I first ate rendang in Amsterdam, where there's a large Malaysian community – it was a knockout: sweet, but not too sweet, spicy, but not too spicy. It's traditionally served with buffalo, slow-cooked to tenderise the meat, and quite dry. Well, I've teamed it with shallots and asparagus and left it a bit wetter, but to be more authentic you can reduce the sauce down.

1 Melt the butter in a pan, add the sugar and when it begins to dissolve chuck in the whole shallots. Season, turn down the heat and cook for at least 45 minutes, turning every 10 minutes or so until the shallots are golden and soft.

2 Blanch the asparagus in boiling salted water, then refresh in ice-cold water.

3 To make the paste, put all the ingredients except the oil in a food processor and blend until smooth.

4 Heat the oil in a wok and fry the paste until fragrant – be careful not to burn it.

5 Add the coconut cream, a little at a time. Then add the coconut milk, bring to the boil and boil to reduce the sauce by half.

6 Add the shallots, asparagus and desiccated coconut and warm through.

7 Garnish with the coriander and serve with jasmine rice.

50g/2oz butter
75g/3oz brown sugar
20 banana shallots
400g/14oz asparagus, trimmed
1 block of coconut cream
400ml tin of coconut milk
50g/2oz toasted desiccated coconut
vegetable oil for frying
salt and freshly ground black pepper
freshly chopped coriander leaves and jasmine rice, to serve

For the paste

1 onion, roughly chopped
2 garlic cloves
2.5cm/1inch piece of fresh ginger
3 red chillies (deseeded if you like)
1 tsp ground coriander
1 tbsp tamarind paste
1 tsp turmeric
1½ tsp curry powder
1 stalk of lemon grass
pinch of salt
2 tbsp vegetable oil for frying

Italian bean casserole

I think there's something very sexy about this dish; we always imagine casseroles to be heavy and robust, but this one has a lightness with a simple tomato base, lots of beans and lemon. Topped with arancini it's hardcore.

1 Heat some oil in a large casserole, add the carrots, celery and leeks and fry for 3–4 minutes. Season and add the garlic and wine. Let the wine cook out and reduce by two-thirds.

2 Tip in the tomatoes and lemon zest and bring to the boil.

3 Add the stock, bring back to the boil and simmer for 20 minutes.

4 Chuck in the beans and cook for 5 minutes, then add the fresh herbs and the lemon juice. It's worth having a quick recheck of the seasoning now.

5 To make the arancini, roll the risotto into 4cm/1½inch balls, press a little cheese into the centre and fold to enclose. Deep-fry in hot oil until golden. Drain on kitchen paper.

6 Serve a good bowlful of casserole with arancini and a little shaved Parmesan on top.

4 carrots, chopped

4 celery stalks, chopped

3 leeks, trimmed, well washed and chopped

2 garlic cloves, crushed

good glug of white wine

400g tin of chopped tomatoes

juice and zest of 1 lemon

200ml/7fl oz fresh stock

100g/3½oz each of cooked borlotti and cannellini beans, drained and rinsed if tinned

fresh oregano

fresh marjoram

olive oil for frying

salt and freshly ground black pepper

Parmesan shavings, to serve

For the arancini

1 quantity cooked tomato risotto (see tomato and mozzarella cakes, page 16)

100g/3½oz mozzarella cheese

vegetable oil for deep-frying

Red Thai bean curry

Once you've mastered the art of making your own Thai curry paste you'll never buy it again. It takes a bit of a shop to get all the gear at first, but all the big supermarkets sell Thai ingredients now, even fresh lime leaves. You won't need all the curry paste, so keep it in an airtight jar in the fridge. Incidentally, try adding a dollop of the paste to creamy mashed potato – divine.

1 To make the curry paste, dry-fry the peppercorns, cumin and coriander seeds until fragrant, then grind them in a mortar and pestle. Put them with all the other paste ingredients except the oil into a blender and blitz until smooth – it takes a good 5–10 minutes.

2 Warm the oil in a pan and add four good spoonfuls of paste (one per person). Cook on a low heat until it becomes fragrant.

3 Crank up the heat and add the coconut milk and stock and bring to the boil. Boil for 3 minutes.

4 Add the fine and broad beans, onions and tomatoes and simmer for about 4 minutes.

5 Divide the luscious curry between four bowls and garnish with lime wedges and coriander and serve with rice.

400ml tin of coconut milk
100ml/3½fl oz stock
225g/8oz cooked fine beans
225g/8oz cooked broad beans
1 bunch of spring onions, finely chopped
2 tomatoes, chopped
lime wedges and fresh coriander leaves, to serve

For the curry paste

10 black peppercorns
2 tsp cumin seeds
2 tsp coriander seeds
10 red chillies (deseeded if you like)
5 shallots
2 garlic cloves, crushed
piece of fresh ginger
6 stalks of lemon grass
12 kaffir lime leaves
pinch of ground cinnamon
½ tsp turmeric
splash of vegetable oil
splash of chilli oil
1 tbsp palm sugar
salt
2 tbsp vegetable oil for frying

Black bean and aubergine chilli

Feeds 6

You don't expect to see aubergines in a chilli, but their meaty texture together with the strong taste of the black beans and the sneaky addition of chocolate make it a delicious combo.

1 Heat the oil in a pan and fry the aubergines for about 4 minutes, to colour and soften. Remove and drain on kitchen paper.

2 Fry the onions and garlic in the same pan until soft, then add the chillies and cook for 5 minutes.

3 Add the tomatoes, coriander, cumin, cinnamon, bay leaf and aubergines and simmer for 5 minutes.

4 Add the beans, season well and cook for 15 minutes. Stir in the chocolate and serve with grated cheese and/or soured cream.

100ml/3½fl oz vegetable oil

450g/1lb aubergines, cut into 2.5cm/1inch cubes

2 red onions, finely chopped

4 garlic cloves, crushed

10 small red chillies, chopped (deseeded if you like)

2 x 400g tins chopped tomatoes

1 tsp ground coriander

pinch of ground cumin

pinch of ground cinnamon

1 bay leaf

250g/9oz cooked black beans, drained and rinsed if tinned

2 tbsp grated dark 70% cocoa-solids chocolate

vegetable oil for frying

salt and freshly ground black pepper

grated cheese and/or soured cream, to serve

Ojja with sweet potato and okra

This is one of the most bizarre success stories on recent menus. This weird little African dish managed to get voted onto the menu in the absence of anything else we could agree on, and it has been really popular. It's got a heady aroma from the smoked paprika and it gets finished with beaten egg, which makes it really creamy.

1 Preheat the oven to 200°C/400°F/mark 6. Pour some oil in a baking tin and put in the oven to heat up. Put the sweet potato with lots of salt and pepper into the hot oil and roast for about 25 minutes until soft and slightly crisp.

2 Meanwhile, make the ojja. Fry the onions and garlic in oil with some seasoning. When they're soft add a splosh of wine and reduce by two-thirds, then add the paprika and cook for about 3 minutes, stirring all the time.

3 Add the tomato purée and stir for a few minutes, then chuck in the tomatoes and bring to the boil. Pour in the stock and cook for about 25 minutes over a low heat until thickened and reduced. Check the seasoning.

4 Blanch the okra and the beans in boiling water, then refresh in ice-cold water.

5 Cook the rice with the turmeric and some salt according to the packet instructions.

6 Heat some oil in a large frying pan, add the spuds and cook until they start to colour up, then add the beans, okra and ojja and bring to the boil. Beat the eggs, add to the pan and let it begin to cook, then fold it through the mixture and keep folding until it creates a lovely marbled effect through the dish.

7 Just before serving, throw in a load of chopped parsley. The texture should be thick enough so you can spoon this up high, it shouldn't be a sloppy casserole. Serve with rice.

2 golden sweet potatoes, peeled and cut into largish bite-sized pieces

75g/3oz fresh okra

100g/3½oz fresh broad beans

500g/1lb 2oz long-grain rice, rinsed and drained

1 tsp turmeric

2 eggs

lots of freshly chopped parsley

olive oil for frying

salt and freshly ground black pepper

For the ojja

2 onions, sliced

3 garlic cloves, crushed

splash of red wine

1 heaped tbsp smoked paprika – it really needs the smoked stuff, unsmoked doesn't do it

1 tbsp tomato purée

400g tin of chopped tomatoes

150ml/5fl oz stock

Plantain and mango curry

Feeds 4

I can't decide when the best time to eat this dish is – it's a neat little lunchy treat, but also great for party food, and really different because it's bright yellow, and nearly sweet enough for a pud. Anyway try it with fresh warm naan bread – and friends.

1 Slice the plantain into pieces the thickness of a pound coin. Place in a pan of boiling salted water with half the turmeric and cook for 10 minutes, then drain.

2 Fry the nigella or mustard seeds in a little oil until they pop, then add the onion, red chilli, curry leaves and some salt. Cook for 5 minutes over a medium heat, stirring pretty much all the time until the onion is golden.

3 Add the ginger and green chilli and cook for 1 minute.

4 Add the rest of the turmeric and mix well, then take off the heat and slowly fold in the yoghurt, plantain and mango.

5 Put back on the heat for 1 minute. Serve with rice or naan bread.

1 plantain, not too ripe, peeled
2 tsp turmeric
1 tsp nigella seeds (or black mustard seeds)
1 onion, finely sliced
1 dried red chilli
about 25 curry leaves
2.5cm/1inch piece of fresh ginger, finely chopped
I fresh green chilli, deseeded and sliced
400ml/14fl oz natural yoghurt
1 firm mango, peeled and sliced
vegetable oil for frying
salt

Oriental pie

*Sounds strange, cooks up a storm. This is really a shepherd's pie-style dish.
Big strong mushroom flavours, enhanced by oriental spices and topped with
a very Western, creamy mash topping. You can substitute pretty much any
favourite earthy veg for the mushrooms.*

1 Fry the spring onions in a little oil until they wilt. Add all the mushrooms to the
pan and cook for 5 minutes, then add the garlic, ginger, cinnamon and star anise
and cook for 5 minutes more.

2 Add the soy sauce and stock and bring to the boil, then simmer for about
10 minutes to reduce by half.

3 Preheat the oven to 200°C/400°F/mark 6. Pour the mushroom mixture into a
baking dish and add the chick peas.

4 To make the topping, put both mashed potatoes into a saucepan and stir to
combine. Beat in the butter and cream and season well, then warm through
over a low heat.

5 Spoon the mash on top of the mushroom and chickpea mixture and cook in
the oven for 15 minutes. Finish off under the grill to brown the top.

8 spring onions, left whole

250g/9oz Portobello
mushrooms, halved

200g/7oz shiitake mushrooms

1 garlic clove, crushed

2.5cm/1inch piece of fresh ginger,
sliced into matchsticks

1 cinnamon stick

2 star anise

100ml/3½fl oz light soy sauce

100ml/3½fl oz stock

200g/7oz cooked chick peas

vegetable oil for frying

For the topping

200g/7oz mashed potato

200g/7oz mashed sweet potato

150g/5½oz butter

50ml/2fl oz double cream

salt and freshly ground black pepper

Caramelised onion and mustard tart

Feeds 6

A big 'meaty' dish that's great for lunch, with sweet, strong onions, the sharpness of the mustard and crisp shortcrust pastry. I serve this with a tomato salad or chutney.

1 Roll out the pastry on a lightly floured surface to fit a 20cm/8inch tart case, press into the case and chill for 20 minutes.

2 Preheat the oven to 200ºC/400ºF/mark 6. Bake the pastry case for 25–30 minutes until crisp and dry.

3 Meanwhile, melt the butter and oil together over a low heat, then add the onions, garlic and seasoning. Cook the onions very slowly for 30–40 minutes until golden – don't let them burn.

4 Whisk together the whole eggs, egg yolks, mustard and cream and stir in the cooked onions. Remove the tart case from the oven and reduce the heat to 180ºC/350ºF/mark 4. Spoon the filling into the tart case and bake for 20 minutes until set firm and golden.

1 quantity shortcrust pastry (see below)

flour for dusting

50g/2oz butter

1 tbsp vegetable oil

4 large Spanish onions, sliced

1 garlic clove, crushed

2 whole eggs, plus 2 egg yolks

2 tbsp wholegrain mustard

150ml/5fl oz double cream

salt and freshly ground black pepper

Shortcrust pastry

Makes enough for 1 x 25cm/10inch pie dish

1 Put the flour, butter and salt in a food processor and pulse until 'crumby'. Add the milk and egg yolk and pulse until a dough forms.

2 Turn the dough out onto a lightly floured surface and knead for a few minutes, then cover and chill for at least 1 hour.

3 When you're ready to use it, roll the dough out on a floured surface and use as directed.

225g/8oz plain flour, plus extra for dusting

75g/3oz chilled butter, cubed

pinch of salt

50ml/2fl oz milk

1 egg yolk

Jerk-spiced pumpkin pie

Feeds 6

Remember eating loads of vol-au-vents filled with mushrooms at parties? You know they're naff, and that mushroom filling is vile, but you can't help yourself. Well, this is Mr vol-au-vent's cooler elder brother, he's bigger, tastier and a whole lot more handsome.

1 Preheat the oven to 190ºC/375ºF/mark 5. Cut a 7.5cm/3inch circle out of the middle of six of the pastry circles. Put the whole pastry circles on a floured baking sheet and sit a cut one on top of each. Brush with eggwash and bake for about 20 minutes until golden brown and dry. Remove the pie cases from the oven.

2 For the filling, pour some oil in a tin and heat to smoking, either in the oven or on the hob. Throw in the squash (not literally!) and shake around for a couple of minutes, then sprinkle on the jerk seasoning and mix well. Roast in the oven for about 25 minutes until soft with a little crispness on the outside. Remove from the tin and put to one side. Pour the oil into a pan and fry the spinach and almonds, then season and add to the squash. Divide the filling between the pie cases and warm through in the oven for 5 minutes.

3 For the curry sauce, heat the oil in a pan and fry the paste until fragrant, then add the coconut milk and stock, bring to the boil and simmer for 5 minutes.

4 Fry the plantain slices gently in oil until golden on each side, then keep them warm.

5 Sit a pie on each plate, spoon over just enough sauce to cover the ingredients, not to swamp them, top with a few slices of the plantain and garnish with coriander.

12 x 15cm/6inch circles of
ready-rolled puff pastry
flour for dusting
2 eggs, beaten, for eggwash
2 plantain, peeled and sliced
vegetable oil for roasting and frying
fresh coriander leaves, to garnish

For the filling

600g/1lb 5oz butternut squash,
peeled and cubed
3 heaped tbsp jerk seasoning
a handful of spinach leaves, well
washed and drained
100g/3½oz toasted flaked almonds
salt and freshly ground black pepper

For the curry sauce

1 tbsp vegetable oil
3 heaped tbsp mild curry paste
400ml tin of coconut milk
100ml/3½fl oz stock

Stilton, asparagus and caramelised shallot roulade with spicy chutney

Feeds 4

This roulade couldn't be more different in flavours than the following one. I've served it with a pear chutney, but I think it's a good dish for Christmas, so try adding a few fresh cranberries to the chutney.

1 First make the roulade. Melt the butter in a pan and stir in the flour to make a roux. Cook for 3 minutes, then add the milk, a little at a time, and stir until thickened. Season well, then stir in the egg yolks. Take off the heat and leave to cool. When cooled, stir in the spinach. Beat the egg whites until stiff then gently fold into the mixture.

2 Preheat the oven to 200°C/400°F/mark 6. Grease and line a 38 x 25cm/15 x 10inch baking tray and sprinkle with flour. Spoon the mixture onto the tray and cook for about 15 minutes until firm and springy. Turn out onto a piece of greaseproof paper, carefully remove the lining paper and leave to cool.

3 For the filling, heat the butter in a pan and when bubbling add the shallots, season well and simmer on a very low heat for 30–40 minutes until rich and golden. Stir frequently to stop them burning. Spread the cream cheese evenly over each cooled roulade, then sprinkle on the Stilton, shallots, nuts and asparagus.

4 Using the greaseproof paper to help you, roll the roulade up from one long side, then wrap in greaseproof paper and foil and chill overnight.

5 To make the chutney, heat a little oil in a pan and fry the shallots and garlic until soft. Add the pears and ginger and cook for 5 minutes, then add the vinegar, sugar and chilli and cook over a low heat for about 20 minutes. Season to taste, then set aside to cool.

6 When ready to serve, preheat the oven to 200°C/400°F/mark 6. Cut the roulade into 8 slices and put on a baking tray. Cook for about 10 minutes until they begin to crisp and brown. Serve the roulade with the chutney and some wilted spinach.

65g/2½oz butter, plus
extra for greasing
100g/3½oz plain flour, plus
extra for dusting
425ml/15fl oz warmed milk
7 eggs, separated
handful of freshly chopped
spinach leaves
salt and freshly ground black pepper

For the filling

50g/2oz butter
15 shallots, sliced
250g/9oz soft cream cheese
150g/5½oz Stilton cheese, crumbled
50g/2oz walnut halves
about 10 asparagus spears, halved
lengthways

For the chutney

olive oil for frying
2 shallots, chopped
1 garlic clove, crushed
6 unpeeled pears, cored and chopped
50g/2oz preserved ginger, chopped
100ml/3½fl oz white wine vinegar
75g/3oz caster sugar
1 chilli, finely chopped

Basil roulade with goat's cheese and sun-blushed tomatoes

Feeds 4

A particularly popular dish whenever it's on the menu at Greens. The combination of goat's cheese, sun-blushed tomatoes and basil makes everyone think of the Mediterranean. But just so you don't get too carried away, some good old British beetroot will bring you back to earth.

Make these roulades a day in advance, so they get a chance to firm up. This is a lovely dish to serve for a special occasion.

1 First make the roulade. Melt the butter in a pan and stir in the flour to make a roux. Cook for 3 minutes, then add the milk, a little at a time, and stir until thickened. Season well, then stir in the egg yolks. Take off the heat and leave to cool.

2 Beat the egg whites until stiff, then gently and carefully fold into the cooled mixture, keeping in as much air as possible. Then gently fold in the basil.

3 Preheat the oven to 200°C/400°F/mark 6. Grease and line a 38 x 25cm/15 x 10inch baking tray. Spread the mixture onto the tray, top with the Parmesan and cook for 15 minutes until springy and risen. Turn out onto a piece of greaseproof paper, carefully remove the lining paper and leave to cool.

4 To make the filling, season the ricotta cheese and spread some on the cooled roulade base, leaving a gap at each end, then sprinkle on the goat's cheese, basil and tomatoes. Roll the roulade up from one long side, then wrap in greaseproof paper and foil and chill overnight.

5 When ready to serve, preheat the oven to 200°C/400°F/mark 6. Slice the roulade, allowing two wedges per person, and heat in the oven for about 10 minutes, then finish off under a hot grill to crisp slightly. Transfer to a serving plate with some watercress.

6 Meanwhile, make the beetroot caviar. Heat the oil in a pan and fry the shallots, garlic and lime leaves until soft, then add the beetroots and warm through. Put into a food processor and pulse until broken down but still a little chunky. Serve with the roulade.

65g/2½oz butter, plus extra
for greasing
100g/3½oz plain flour
425ml/15fl oz milk, warmed
7 eggs, separated
big handful of roughly chopped
fresh basil leaves
75g/3oz freshly grated
Parmesan cheese
salt and freshly ground black pepper
watercress, to serve

For the filling

250g/9oz ricotta cheese
100g/3½oz goat's cheese, crumbled
big handful of fresh basil leaves
sprinkle of sun-blushed tomatoes

For the beetroot caviar

25ml/1fl oz olive oil
2 shallots, finely chopped
1 garlic clove, crushed
4 lime leaves, shredded
6 cooked beetroots, peeled and
chopped

Side dishes

Bubble and squeak

Feeds 4

*I've heard rumours of people using cabbage, rather than sprouts, in their bubble…
you, of course, would never dream of such a barbaric act. Long live the sprouts!*

1 Fry the onions in half the butter until soft, but not coloured. Leave to cool.

2 Combine the onions with the spuds, sprouts and garlic and season well (heavy on
the pepper).

3 Divide the mix into four and shape into squares or rounds. Dust with a little flour and
fry in the remaining butter for about 5 minutes on each side until golden.

2 onions, sliced
50g/2oz butter
200g/7oz mashed spuds (no
butter or cream)
200g/7oz cooked sprouts
1 garlic clove, crushed
a little flour for dusting
salt and freshly ground black pepper

Pan haggerty

Feeds 4

*I hope this version of the classic north-east potato dish is accurate, otherwise
Scotty and all my Geordie mates will never forgive me. It's a great side dish for
a lazy Sunday supper.*

1 Preheat the oven to 180ºC/350ºF/mark 4. Heat half the butter in an ovenproof
pan and fry the onion until soft, then remove from the pan.

2 Put a layer of potato in the same pan and fry for a few minutes until golden.

3 Now layer up onion, potato, onion, seasoning each layer and finishing with potato.

4 Melt the remaining butter and pour over the pan. Cook in the oven for about
40 minutes until soft.

5 Before serving, grate the cheese over the top and put under a hot grill until
the cheese bubbles.

50g/2oz butter
1 onion, finely sliced
200g/7oz waxy potatoes, peeled and
finely sliced
75g/3oz mature Cheddar cheese
salt and freshly ground black pepper

Lentils with lemon

So often lentils get overcooked and taste of nothing, but this dish uses Puy lentils, which are a lovely green lentil when cooked, but a bluey/purple when raw. Adding lemon and red peppers makes this a yummy dish to serve on the side of just about everything savoury.

1 Boil the lentils for 10 minutes in lots of boiling salted water. Drain.

2 Bring the stock to the boil and add the lentils and garlic. When it returns to the boil chuck in the lemon juice, zest and the peppers. Adjust the seasoning and serve immediately.

175g/6oz Puy lentils

75ml/3fl oz stock

1 garlic clove, crushed

juice and zest of 1 lemon

½ red pepper, deseeded and finely diced

salt and freshly ground black pepper

Smoky roasties

Enough for you – and 3 others

You can't beat a good roastie, crisp on the outside, fluffy on the inside and nice and salty. Well, these chaps are so good you can eat them on their own. I'd keep these a secret from all of your friends, otherwise you'll become a roast potato factory.

1 Preheat the oven to 220ºC/425ºF/mark 7. Pour the oil into an ovenproof dish and heat to smoking in the oven.

2 Cut the spuds into big chunks, about 5cm/2inch-ish in an abstract way. Boil them for 4 minutes in salted water, then drain and return them to the pan. Pop them back on the heat and give them a good shake (this will break up the edges and give them that crispy/fluffy look) for a minute or so.

3 Remove the hot oil from the oven, lift the spuds out of the pan, ignoring all the small 'crumbs', and pop them into the oil. Put them straight in the oven and cook, turning them every 10–15 minutes, for 30 minutes until crisp and golden.

4 Just before serving, season them with salt, sprinkle on the paprika, give 'em another gentle shake and serve.

150ml/5fl oz olive oil

4–6 large, floury spuds, peeled

sea salt

good pinch of smoked paprika

Sprouts with beetroot

Feeds 4

Two of the most maligned and underrated veggies in the world. Sprouts aren't just for Christmas and beetroot isn't just to be pickled in a jar. The combination of these two is heavenly – sweet, sharp and with garlic and chilli thrown in. Don't be afraid, try them.

1 Preheat the oven to 200°C/400°F/mark 6. Season the beetroots, wrap them in foil and roast for about 40 minutes until soft. Allow to cool, then peel them and cut into wedges.

2 If the sprouts are big, cut them in half, if not, leave them whole.

3 Heat the oil in a frying pan until hot. Simply chuck in the sprouts, let them fry for a minute to begin browning, then give them a shake.

4 Now put the beetroot, chilli and garlic into the pan. Cook for a couple of minutes, then season really well.

5 Serve as a funky veg.

2 raw beetroot
300g/10½oz cooked sprouts
a little olive oil for frying
pinch of chilli flakes
1 garlic clove, crushed
salt and freshly ground black pepper

Glazed carrots with caraway seeds

Feeds 4

If you're bored with carrots, then tuck into these tasty, sweet little beauties.

1 Pop the carrots in a pan with a good pinch of salt and just cover them with water. Add the sugar, caraway and butter, bring to the boil and simmer for 8–10 minutes, until just tender, but with a bite.

2 Drain the liquid into another pan and reduce by about two-thirds.

3 Add the carrots and caraway to the pan, season and serve.

450g/1lb peeled carrots, cut into batons
1 tsp sugar
1 tsp caraway seeds
40g/1½oz butter
salt and freshly ground black pepper

Stuffed pimentos with thyme and basil

Feeds 4

If you're serving something quite plain, then these sweet, slightly spicy peppers are a great accompaniment. Because they get charred and the thyme and basil are pretty strong they make the most boring dish spring to life.

1 Heat a griddle pan to smoking hot and brush it with a tiny amount of oil. Griddle the peppers on both sides until lightly charred. Meanwhile, mix together the ricotta, thyme, lemon juice and seasoning.

2 While the peppers are still warm, roughly spread a spoonful of the mix onto each pepper. Sit the peppers side by side on a plate, sprinkle a few basil leaves on top and serve (if you want a bit more spice, drizzle a little chilli oil over the peppers before serving).

a little vegetable or olive oil for griddling
6 long thin red pimento peppers, halved lengthways and deseeded
175g/6oz ricotta cheese
small bunch of fresh thyme
juice of ½ lemon
a few fresh basil leaves
salt and freshly ground black pepper

Celeriac and potato dauphinoise

Feeds 6

It's a grand tradition Chez Rimmer to have dauphinoise potatoes to excess at Christmas time, so imagine everyone's surprise when that tasty, yet ugly veg the celeriac joined the celebrations. But let me tell you, he was a most welcome guest after the first large mouthful as celeriac is a brilliant addition to your creamy dauphinoise.

1 Heat the butter in a pan and gently fry the onion and garlic until soft, but not brown. Reserve a little of the cheese, then layer up the spuds, celeriac, remaining cheese and onion in a buttered baking dish, seasoning each layer as you go. Combine the creams and season well, then pour into the dish and leave to stand for about 20 minutes.

2 Preheat the oven to 170ºC/325ºF/mark 3. Sprinkle the dish with the reserved cheese, then cook the dauphinoise for about 1½ hours until soft.

25g/1oz butter, plus extra for greasing
1 onion, finely sliced
1 garlic clove, crushed
150g/5½oz mature Cheddar cheese, grated
450g/1lb floury spuds, peeled and finely sliced
450g/1lb celeriac, peeled and finely sliced
285ml carton double cream
285ml carton single cream
salt and freshly ground black pepper

Parmesan-roasted parsnips

Feeds 6, if you're lucky

I adore all roasted veg, but parsnips are just about my faves. Adding strong Parmesan and garlic makes them good enough to eat on their own – so if you're serving these as a veg with your roast make twice the amount because you'll eat half of them before they get to the table.

1 Preheat the oven to 220ºC/425ºF/mark 7. Pour some oil into a roasting tin and put in the oven to heat up. Toss the parsnips in the garlic and seasoning.

2 When the oil is smoking, add the parsnips to the tin and roast for about 25 minutes, shaking occasionally (that's the parsnips, not you).

3 Then add the cheese and roast for another 10 minutes. The cheese will begin to melt and form a yummy, stringy coating.

4 Serve the parsnips topped with a twist of black pepper and a little chopped parsley.

400g/14oz parsnips, peeled and cut into 5cm/2inch batons
1 garlic clove, sliced
150g/5½oz freshly grated Parmesan cheese
olive oil for roasting
salt and freshly ground black pepper
freshly chopped parsley, to serve

Fine beans with garlic and tomato sauce

Feeds 6

Fine beans are one of the few veg that I like cooked slowly; they become deliciously sweet and scrummy. Add a touch of cinnamon to the tomato sauce for an extra flavour.

1 Preheat the oven to 170ºC/325ºF/mark 3. Cook the beans in boiling salted water for about 4 minutes, then refresh in ice-cold water.

2 Heat the oil in an ovenproof dish, add the garlic and as soon as it begins to 'fizz' add the beans and tomato sauce. Season well and stir to mix, then cook in the oven for 25 minutes until the beans are soft and sweet.

450g/1lb fine beans
100ml/3½fl oz olive oil
4 garlic cloves, sliced
250ml/9fl oz basic tomato sauce (see page 107)
salt and freshly ground black pepper

Coconut rice in banana leaf

Feeds 6

There's a good few curries in the book, so this is a simple, yet effective way to serve rice. Good to put on the barbie as well.

1 Put the rice in a pan with the water and coconut cream. Bring to the boil and cook for about 12 minutes.

2 Take it off the heat and stir in the chillies. Divide between the banana leaves, top with some coriander and wrap the leaves up. Secure the leaf parcels with a skewer then put in a steamer and steam for another 5 minutes.

225g/8oz long-grain
rice, rinsed and drained
450ml/16fl oz water
225g/8oz block coconut
cream, chopped
2 small red chillies,
deseeded and sliced
6 pieces banana leaf, about
30 x 20cm/12 x 8inches
fresh coriander leaves

Basic tomato sauce

Makes enough sauce for 4 large
bowls of pasta

I prefer this slightly heavier tomato sauce for my dishes as that little bit of extra depth helps with a lot of veggie food. I recommend making twice this amount if you use it on a regular basis, as you can freeze it and use at a later date.

1 Heat the oil in a large pan and gently fry the onion, celery and garlic until soft.

2 Add the tomato purée and cook for a few minutes, then add the tomatoes, stock and wine. Season and bring to the boil.

3 Turn the heat right down, half cover the pan and simmer for about 1 hour, stirring every now and again.

4 If you want a nice smooth sauce blend in a processor and pass through a fine sieve before using, otherwise use as is.

100ml/3½fl oz olive oil
1 onion, chopped
1 celery stalk, finely chopped
2 garlic cloves, chopped
2 tbsp tomato purée
2 x 400g tins chopped tomatoes
100ml/3½fl oz stock
100ml/3½fl oz red wine
salt and freshly ground black pepper

Puddings

Ice-lollies

Remember when you were a kid and you made simple lollies from orange squash that was always a bit too strong, so it made you cough? Well, now is the time to rediscover your childhood and make these two yummy lollies that kids will love, but that are a great fun thing to have at a summer party. Serve them in a bowl of ice with the sticks pointing up.

Watermelon and lime

Makes 8 lollies

Put the sugar, water and vanilla seeds into a pan and heat until the sugar dissolves, then cool and chill until really cold. Stir in the watermelon and lime juices, pour into eight lolly moulds and freeze. Don't forget the sticks.

125g/4½oz caster sugar

125ml/4fl oz water

seeds of 1 vanilla pod

about 600ml/1 pint watermelon juice
(squeeze out some watermelon pulp)

juice of 2 limes

Strawberry and black pepper lolly

Makes 8 lollies

Simply blend the yoghurt, fruit and sugar together, then add a good twist of pepper. Pour into moulds and freeze. Don't forget the sticks.

300ml/10fl oz natural yoghurt

125g/4½oz strawberries, hulled

50g/2oz caster sugar

freshly ground black pepper

Honeycomb ice cream

Feeds 6

The taste of honeycomb/cinder toffee is divine, a real taste of childhood, and I even like the 3 hours it takes to pick the bits out of my teeth. Well, it's only very recently that I learned how to make it and now I can't stop, much to the delight of my dentist, Roger. I have to confess that this is based hugely on a recipe by Thane Prince.

If you've tried making ice cream before and been disappointed by the results because it's too 'icy', well this is a creamy winner – the secret ingredient is vodka, which has a lower freezing point and stops those ice-crystals forming. Now, where did I put that toothpick?

1 To make the honeycomb, put the sugar and syrup into a pan and warm until the sugar dissolves, then turn up the heat until it starts to form a caramel. The longer you leave it the more caramelly it becomes, but don't leave it too long as it'll burn. You want it golden.

2 Now, chuck in the bicarbonate of soda and stir well, then pour onto a greased tray and allow to cool (how easy is that?).

3 For the ice cream, whip the cream until it becomes thick, but not fully whipped. Fold in the vodka and condensed milk and whisk until firm, then break in the honeycomb and mix well. Pour into a freezer container and freeze for at least 8 hours – there's no need to churn.

For the honeycomb

75g/3oz caster sugar

2 tbsp golden syrup

2 tbsp bicarbonate of soda, sifted

For the ice cream

600ml/1 pint double cream

3 tbsp vodka

200ml/7fl oz condensed milk

Strawberry soup

Feeds 4–6

This is a really lovely summer dessert, full of flavour and colour. The best way to describe the taste is like a good snog! – and your lips tingle afterwards.

1 Put 800g/1¾lb of the strawberries and all the caster sugar in a food processor and process to a purée. Pass through a sieve into a serving bowl and stir in the wine.

2 Add the nectarines, raspberries and the pulp from the passion fruit and stir to mix.

3 Cover and chill until lovely and cold.

4 Serve each helping with a quenelle of mascarpone and fresh mint leaves.

1kg/2¼lb strawberries, hulled
75g/3oz caster sugar
100ml/3½fl oz dessert wine
2 nectarines, peeled and diced
250g/9oz raspberries, halved
4 passion fruit, halved
100g/3½oz mascarpone cheese
mint leaves, to garnish

Strawberry, vodka and black pepper granita

Feeds 6

This isn't really a pudding but I wanted to include it as it's a great drink to start or end a summer evening with – fruity, boozy and refreshing, and lethal!

1 Heat the sugar and water in a saucepan over a low heat until the sugar dissolves, then take off the heat and chill.

2 Blend the chilled syrup with the fuit, booze and pepper.

3 Pour into a freezer container, then put in the freezer.

4 Break up the ice crystals every 40 minutes until the granita is completely frozen and has a grainy consistency.

5 Serve in chilled stem glasses with more fruit and mint.

500g/1lb 2oz caster sugar
500ml/18fl oz water
300g/10½oz strawberries, plus extra to decorate
100ml/3½fl oz vodka
good twist black pepper
fresh mint leaves, to garnish

Strawberry and coconut trifle

Makes 6 individual or 1 big trifle

I love trifle, it always reminds me of big family parties when I was a kid. You just can't beat sherry-soaked cake, trapped inside jelly with a big load of tinned fruit, topped with custard, cream and then decorated with hundreds and thousands and those little silver balls that break your teeth in half. Now this trifle is so gorgeous you'll want to stick pictures of it in a scrapbook and send it fan mail. Making custard with coconut milk really is spectacular, while soaking fat juicy strawberries in Cointreau is making me salivate as I write. Anyway, to the recipe.

This does take a bit of time as you've got to make the custard and then let it cool, so if you're thinking of making it for tea tonight, better eat late.

1 First make the custard. Whisk the egg yolks and sugar until they're pale and creamy, then sift in the flour and mix well. Put the coconut milk and vanilla seeds into another pan and very slowly bring it to the boil (if you want a really thick custard use just the top solid part of the coconut milk, you'll need 2 tins). When it's come to the boil, take it off the heat, pour over the egg mixture and whisk well. Pour it all back into the pan and bring back up to the boil, then simmer for 5 minutes, stirring all the time. Take it off the heat again, pour into a bowl, cover with cling film and chill. When it's cold, whip the cream and fold in. Have a sneaky taste of it – how good?

2 Meanwhile, put the strawberries into a bowl, cover with icing sugar and Cointreau and chill them for about 1 hour. Break the cake up into chunks and either line the bottom of a big glass bowl or divide into six glasses or little bowls. (I like it both ways, but I do love that slurping sound when you spoon a big portion out of a large bowl.) Splash some Cointreau over the cake.

3 Tip the strawberries on top of the cake, then the kiwi slices. Warm the jam with a little water to soften it, then pour it over the cake and fruit. Spoon all the chilled custard onto the cake and fruit.

4 To make the topping, whip the cream and mix with the mascarpone, then spoon over the custard. Finally, sprinkle the toasted coconut on top and serve – you'll never buy a packet trifle again.

400g/14oz strawberries, hulled and chopped into good-sized chunks
50g/2oz icing sugar
good glugs of Cointreau
about 250g/9oz cake, Madeira, Swiss roll, muffins – all work well
2 kiwi fruit, peeled and sliced
250g/9oz strawberry jam

For the custard

6 egg yolks
125g/4½oz caster sugar
40g/1½oz plain flour
400ml tin of coconut milk
seeds of 1 vanilla pod
200ml/7fl oz double cream

For the topping

100ml/3½fl oz whipping cream
100g/3½oz mascarpone cheese
50g/2oz desiccated coconut, toasted

Cherry tiramisu cheesecake

Feeds 12

This combines black forest gâteau with a tiramisu, both of which have become a bit naff in recent times, so the only way to rescue them is to turn them into cheesecake!

1 To make the base, put the biscuits, butter and sugar into a bowl and combine well, then press into a 23cm/9inch springform tin and chill for 20 minutes.

2 Preheat the oven to 180°C/350°F/mark 4. Drain the cherries and reserve the juice. Put the juice and booze in a small saucepan and bring to the boil. Combine the cornflour with a little water to make a paste, then add to the liquid. This will thicken it to a 'jam'. Cook over a low heat for a couple of minutes, then pour over the cherries and stir to combine. Place a few cherries on the biscuit base.

3 To make the topping, beat the cheeses together with the sugar and vanilla, then fold in the eggs, one at a time. Finally, stir in the chocolate and pour onto the biscuit base. Bake in the oven for 45–60 minutes, until the top is firm yet yielding. Remove and cool.

4 For the sauce, simply mix the water, syrup and butter into the chocolate.

5 To serve, spoon the rest of the cherries over the top of the cheesecake, cut a big slab, sit it on a plate with choccy sauce and cream and enjoy.

For the base

225g/8oz crushed water biscuits
150g/5½oz unsalted butter, melted
100g/3½oz soft brown sugar

For the filling

200g tin of black cherries
splash of Kirsch
a little cornflour

For the topping

700g/1lb 9oz ricotta cheese
200g/7oz mascarpone cheese
150g/5½oz caster sugar
dash of vanilla extract
6 eggs
250g/9oz dark 70% cocoa-solids chocolate, melted

For the sauce

4 tbsp water
1 tbsp golden syrup
15g/½oz unsalted butter
150g/5½oz dark 70% cocoa-solids chocolate, melted
cream, to serve

Zucotto

Remember when you couldn't move for tiramisu on restaurant menus? It always amazed me that this cracking cream- and choccy-filled dessert didn't make it into our psyche then too – maybe now is the time. Spread the word: zucotto is king.

1 Line a 1.5 litre/2½ pint round-bottomed bowl or basin with clingfilm. Mix the brandy, orange liqueur and orange juice together in a separate bowl and dip the cake slices in it. Line the bowl or basin with three-quarters of the moist cake slices until all the inside is covered.

2 Fold the icing sugar into the cream.

3 Grate half the chocolate and mix with all the nuts and three-quarters of the cream. Spread over the cake slices in the basin, then mould a hollow in the middle.

4 Melt the remaining chocolate and stir into the rest of the cream. Put this in the hollow and smooth.

5 Cover the cream with the remaining moist cake slices, then cover and chill for 24 hours.

6 Turn the cake out onto a plate, pour over some melted chocolate, then cut generous pieces and eat with yet more cream.

3 tbsp brandy

2 tbsp orange liqueur

5 tbsp fresh orange juice

2 shop-bought Madeira cakes, trimmed and cut into slices

100g/3½oz icing sugar

450ml/16fl oz double cream, whipped

150g/5½oz dark 70% cocoa-solids chocolate

50g/2oz flaked, toasted almonds

50g/2oz roasted skinned hazelnuts

melted chocolate and cream, to serve

Peanut butter and 'jelly' cheesecake

This is a real 'love or hate' recipe; for me the combo is so American. If you can get hold of it, use Skippy supercrunch peanut butter, it has a taste and texture like no other. If you can't, the next time a friend is going to the States get them to stock up for you.

1 To make the base, put the biccies and butter into a bowl, combine well and press into a 23cm/9inch springform tin. Chill for 20 minutes.

2 Preheat the oven to 180°C/350°F/mark 4. For the topping, just put the cheese, sugar, eggs and vanilla into a blender and pulse until smooth. Don't worry if the mix seems a bit runny, the eggs will set it.

3 Spoon the mixture into a bowl and fold in the peanut butter.

4 Spread the jam over the biscuit base, leaving about a 2.5cm/1inch gap all the way round, then spoon the peanut mixture on top.

5 Bake in the oven for about 1 hour. The cheesecake should be springy and just set in the middle. If you can turn off the oven and leave the cake in with the door just open until cool, this will help to stop it cracking, but it's not crucial as it'll get eaten straight away once it's cool.

For the base

200g/7oz crushed digestive biccies

150g/5½oz unsalted butter, melted

For the topping

600g/1lb 5oz full-fat cream cheese

150g/5½oz caster sugar

6 eggs

splash of vanilla extract

150g/5½oz crunchy peanut butter

150g/5½oz strawberry jam

Lychee and toasted coconut cheesecake

Feeds 12

As you know, I love Asian food, but their lack of dairy makes the desserts a bit disappointing for Western palates, so this member of my cheesecake family uses lovely Asian influences in our favourite pud. This is lovely served with mango kulfi or lime sorbet.

1 Usual base job: combine the biccies, sugar and butter. Press into a 23cm/9inch springform tin and chill for 20 minutes.

2 Preheat the oven to 180°C/350°F/mark 4. Put the coconut under a hot grill and shake around until it's toasted and golden. Don't even think about leaving it as I guarantee you'll burn it – I always do and so do my team.

3 Put the cheese and sugar into a food processor and pulse together, then add the eggs and pulse to combine.

4 Tip the mixture into a large bowl and fold in the lychees and 100g/3½oz of the coconut. Spoon onto the biscuit base, then sprinkle over the remaining coconut.

5 Bake in the oven for about 1 hour. You're looking for a cake that's firm yet yielding! Allow to cool before serving.

For the base

250g/9oz crushed water biscuits
100g/3½oz soft light brown sugar
150g/5½oz unsalted butter, melted

For the filling

150g/5½oz desiccated coconut
900g/2lb cream cheese
150g/5½oz caster sugar
6 eggs
400g tin of lychees, drained, or
12 fresh, peeled and stoned

More chocolate than is good for you

I recommend you make this for someone you fancy – wife, husband, girlfriend, lover, Britney Spears. As long as they love choccy, I guarantee they will be powerless to your advances as the god of luurve of cheesecakes takes control.

1 Crush the bourbon biscuits, add the butter and mix well, then press into a 23cm/9inch springform tin and chill for 20 minutes.

2 Preheat the oven to 180ºC/350ºF/mark 4. To make the filling, put the chocolate in a bowl over barely simmering water (make sure the water doesn't touch the bottom of the bowl) and leave until melted.

3 Put the cream cheese and caster sugar in a food processor and whiz until smooth, then add the eggs and pulse to mix. Add the cocoa powder and melted chocolate and pulse again.

4 Spoon the filling onto the biscuit base and cook in the oven for about 1 hour until springy to the touch. Allow to cool in the tin then turn it out.

5 Ideally this should be served topped with grated chocolate, a dusting of cocoa powder and with a rich chocolate sauce. To make the sauce, melt the chocolate and cream over a bowl of simmering water, then whisk in the butter. (Serve the sauce immediately as it won't reheat.) Now wait for the magic to work.

For the base

250g/9oz bourbon biscuits

125g/4½oz unsalted butter, melted

For the filling

200g/7oz dark 70% cocoa-solids chocolate

900g/2lb full-fat cream cheese

150g/5½oz golden caster sugar

6 eggs

75g/3oz cocoa powder, plus extra for dusting

For the sauce

225g/8oz dark 70% cocoa-solids chocolate, plus extra for sprinkling

250ml/9fl oz double cream

25g/1oz unsalted butter, cut into small pieces

Goat's cheese and lemon cheesecake

This is a brilliant dessert for anyone without a hugely sweet tooth, the strong goat's cheese works brilliantly with the lemon; it's the only slightly grown-up one of all the cheesecakes.

1 To make the base, put the biccies, nuts and butter into a bowl, mix together and press into a 23cm/9inch springform tin. Chill for 20 minutes.

2 Preheat the oven to 180°C/350°F/mark 4. Pop both cheeses and the sugar into a food processor and pulse till smoothish. I like a bit of texture in this one.

3 Add the eggs and lemon zest and juice and pulse to combine, then spoon onto the biscuit base. Bake in the oven for about 1 hour until the cake is springy. Let it cool fully before turning out. I like to serve this with Greek yoghurt, rather than cream.

For the base

200g/7oz crushed water biscuits

50g/2oz crushed pecans

125g/4½oz unsalted butter, melted

For the filling

600g/1lb 5oz peeled goat's cheese

300g/10½oz mascarpone cheese

150g/5½oz caster sugar

6 eggs

zest and juice of 2 lemons

Pecan and white chocolate pie

Feeds 12

While I love the sophistication of a classic lemon tart and the delights of summer fruits, I think a piece of pie is second only to cheesecake in the pudding stakes. Pecan pie is a sugar junkies' delight. To make it richer I'm adding white chocolate.

1 Preheat the oven to 200°C/400°F/mark 6. Roll out the pastry on a lightly floured surface and press it into a 25cm/10inch tart case. Line the pastry with foil and rice or baking beans and bake in the oven for 15 minutes. Then remove the rice and foil and cook for another 15 minutes to dry out the case.

2 Beat one of the eggs and brush the pastry case with this eggwash, then cook for a further 5 minutes to seal the case.

3 Meanwhile, make the filling. Whisk the remaining eggs well, then add the sugar, syrup, butter and vanilla and mix well.

4 Lightly break half the nuts and fold into the mixture, together with the chocolate. Pour the mix into the cooked case and then top with the remaining nuts.

5 Reduce the oven to 180°C/350°F/mark 4 and bake the pie for 40 minutes until set (don't panic if the mixture looks too sloppy – it will set it fast). Leave the pie to cool.

6 Serve a large wedge with a spoonful of wicked clotted cream.

1 quantity of sweet shortcrust pastry (see page 124)
flour for dusting
7 eggs
225g/8oz soft light brown sugar
150g/5½oz golden syrup
50g/2oz unsalted butter, melted
a dash of vanilla extract
450g/1lb shelled pecan nuts
100g/3½oz white chocolate, grated
clotted cream, to serve

Passion fruit tart

If you like classic French lemon tart, then you're gonna love this baby. The exotic taste of passion fruit is magnificent. In fact, the passion fruit syrup is a great sweet sauce for ice creams and poured over fruit.

1 To make the pastry, put the flour, butter, salt and icing sugar in a food processor and pulse until 'crumby'. Add the milk and egg yolks and pulse until it forms a dough. Turn it out onto a floured surface and knead for a few minutes, then cover and chill for at least 1 hour.

2 Turn the pastry out onto your floured surface and roll out 5cm/2inches larger than a 28cm/11inch tart case. Push the pastry into the base, leaving the excess hanging over the sides, and chill for at least 30 minutes.

3 Preheat the oven to 180°C/350°F/mark 4. Line the pastry case with foil and rice or baking beans and bake in the oven for 20 minutes. Remove the rice or beans and foil, brush with the eggwash and cook for a further 10 minutes. Remove from the oven and trim off the excess pastry with a sharp knife. Leave to cool.

4 To make the filling, put the sugar and water into a saucepan and heat gently until the sugar dissolves. Tip in the passion fruit pulp and allow to cool.

5 Whisk the eggs and sugar together, then add the cream. Using a slotted spoon, add all the passion fruit pulp to the cream mixture with a little of the juice, probably about 1 tablespoon. Reserve the remaining juice to use as extra sauce.

6 Pour this custard into the cooked and cooled tart case. Incidentally, a little tip is to fill the tart case while it's sitting on the oven shelf, with the shelf pulled out – genius or what?

7 Reduce the oven to 170°C/325°F/mark 3 and bake the tart on the middle shelf for about 40 minutes. It should still be a little wobbly, but it will carry on cooking and will set. To serve, dust the tart with icing sugar and a spoonful of the extra sauce.

For the pastry

225g/8oz plain flour, plus
extra for dusting

75g/3oz cold unsalted butter, cubed

pinch of salt

100g/3½oz sifted icing sugar

50ml/2fl oz milk

2 egg yolks

1 egg, beaten, for eggwash

icing sugar, to serve

For the filling

350g/12oz caster sugar

150ml/5fl oz water

pulp and juice of 12 passion fruit

9 eggs

300ml/10fl oz double cream

Chocolate and prune tart with Earl Grey tea custard

If you think prunes are something to be avoided at all costs, think again, at least until you've tried this decadent tart. Soaking them in Earl Grey tea overnight brings out a really rich flavour in them, which goes particularly well with chocolate – and brandy.

1 Preheat the oven to 200°C/400°F/mark 6. Roll out the pastry on a lightly floured surface and press it into a 25cm/10inch tart case. Line the pastry with foil and rice or baking beans and bake in the oven for 15 minutes. Then remove the rice and foil and cook for another 15 minutes to dry out the case.

2 Brush the pastry case with the eggwash, then cook for a further 5 minutes to seal the case.

3 To make the filling, strain the prunes and reserve the tea.

4 Put the chocolate and butter into a bowl.

5 Pour the cream into a pan and bring just up to the boil, then pour over the chocolate and butter and stir until it's all smooth and creamy.

6 Pour just enough of the chocolate mixture into the pastry case to leave a little space at the top, then press the prunes into the surface in a jolly attractive manner. Chill to set.

7 To make the custard, heat the milk to scalding point.

8 Whisk the egg yolks and sugar together in a pan, then pour the milk over them and stir to combine. Add the vanilla seeds and about 50ml/2fl oz of the reserved Earl Grey tea and put back on a low heat. Cook, stirring, until the custard will coat the back of a spoon.

9 Cut a big fat piece of tart, sit it on a plate, pour on some custard and have a large brandy.

1 quantity sweet shortcrust pastry (see page 124)
flour for dusting
1 egg, beaten, for eggwash

For the filling

20 Agen prunes, stoned and soaked in Earl Grey tea overnight
300g/10½oz dark 70% cocoa-solids chocolate, broken into pieces
25g/1oz unsalted butter
300ml/10fl oz double cream

For the custard

400ml/14fl oz milk
4 egg yolks
25g/1oz caster sugar
seeds of 1 vanilla pod

Spotted dick with banana and toffee

Feeds 6

School dinners? Lumpy custard? Spotted Dick? I can see how your mind works. Forget all about those memories and join 'puddings re-united'; this is that long-lost friend who was a bit geeky at school, but has grown into a smooth sophisticated professional and is now everyone's best mate. Go on, you know you want to...

1 Put the flour, baking powder, suet, sugar, currants and orange zest into a bowl and stir to mix. Add the milk and bananas and mix to a dough.

2 Roll the dough into a cylinder, about 15 x 5cm/6 x 2inches. Wrap in buttered greaseproof, leaving room for it to rise, and seal at each end. Put into a steamer and steam for 1 hour.

3 To make the custard, put the milk and vanilla seeds into a pan and bring to the boil. Pour onto the egg yolks and sugar and beat well. Return to the pan and cook over a low heat until it coats the back of a spoon.

4 For the toffee sauce, put the sugar, butter and syrup into a pan and bring to the boil, then remove from the heat and add the cream.

5 Unwrap the steamed pudding and cut into slices. Cover with the custard and then the toffee sauce.

300g/10½oz plain flour

2 tsp baking powder

150g/5½oz shredded vegetable suet

75g/3oz caster sugar

100g/3½oz currants

zest of 1 orange

150ml/5fl oz milk

1–2 bananas, chopped

butter for greasing

For the custard

600ml/1 pint milk

seeds of 1 vanilla pod

6 egg yolks

75g/3oz caster sugar

For the toffee sauce

100g/3½oz soft dark brown sugar

100g/3½oz unsalted butter

100g/3½oz golden syrup

100ml/3½fl oz double cream

Melting chocolate pudding

Feeds 4

I feel it my duty to issue a health warning with this magnificent pud – OK, you have to be willing to experience rich banana cake, melting ganache (the stuff in the middle of posh chocolates) as well as creamy, chocolatey custard. This pud is so sexy that if it was a girlfriend you wouldn't take it home to meet your parents! Speaking of which – the banana loaf recipe is my mum's and is brilliant sliced and buttered on its own. Thanks, mum.

1 First make the ganache. Put the chocolate and butter in a bowl. Pour the cream into a pan, add the sugar and bring to the boil, then pour over the chocolate and butter and stir to melt. Cover and chill for at least 4 hours.

2 Preheat the oven to 180°C/350°F/mark 4. Grease a 900g/2lb loaf tin. To make the banana loaf, dissolve the bicarbonate of soda in the milk, then add the bananas. Sift the baking powder and flour together in a large bowl, then fold in the banana mixture. Stir in the butter, sugars and the eggs. Spoon the mixture into the loaf tin and bake for about 1 hour, until set. Allow to cool.

3 To make the custard, put the chocolate, coffee and butter into a bowl. In a separate bowl, whisk together the eggs, egg yolks and sugar. Put the cream and milk into a saucepan, bring to the boil, then pour over the chocolate and coffee mixture and stir to melt. Then pour this over the whisked eggs and sugar and stir to combine.

4 Trim the edges of the banana loaf and cut the loaf into 2.5cm/1inch cubes. Put the cubes in a large bowl, pour enough chocolate custard over to cover them, and leave to stand for 30 minutes.

5 Preheat the oven to 200°C/400°F/mark 6. Butter four rings, 7.5cm/3inch ideally, and stand them on greaseproof paper. Pack each halfway with some of the custardy cake. Roll a ball of ganache and pop it onto the middle of the cake, top with more cake and a little more custard. Bake for 15 minutes and serve immediately with the remaining custard or cream. When you cut open the pud the melted ganache will ooze out.

For the banana loaf

1 tsp bicarbonate of soda

2 tbsp milk

3 mashed bananas

1 tsp baking powder

225g/8oz plain flour

125g/4½oz unsalted butter, softened

50g/2oz brown sugar

100g/3½oz granulated sugar

2 eggs, beaten

For the custard

250g/9oz dark 70% cocoa-solids chocolate, broken into pieces

a shot of strong espresso coffee

50g/2oz unsalted butter

3 eggs and 2 yolks

150g/5½oz brown sugar

300ml/10fl oz double cream

200ml/7fl oz milk

For the ganache

250g/9oz dark 70% cocoa-solids chocolate, broken into pieces

15g/½oz butter

250ml/9fl oz double cream

25g/1oz caster sugar

Chocolate brownies with marshmallow sauce

Feeds 4

Are they a cake or a biscuit? I can never decide, so I constantly eat them to try and make up my mind. These fellas are really rich and the melty, marshmallow sauce is like eating liquid fluffy clouds.

1 Preheat the oven to 180°C/350°F/mark 4. Put the eggs and sugar in a bowl and beat until pale and creamy, then add the butter.

2 Sift the flour and cocoa into the egg mixture, then add the melted choccy and the nuts and mix well.

3 Spoon the mixture into a greased 20cm/8inch baking dish and bake in the oven for about 35 minutes. Allow to cool.

4 To make the sauce, bring the cream and vanilla to the boil, then simmer for 5 minutes to thicken. Now stir in the marshmallows. The sauce is ready when the marshmallows are half melted.

5 Cut a decent chunk of brownie and pour over the liquid clouds!

4 eggs

225g/8oz caster sugar

225g/8oz unsalted butter, melted, plus extra for greasing

75g/3oz plain flour

75g/3oz cocoa powder

225g/8oz dark 70% cocoa-solids chocolate, melted

100g/3½oz chopped skinned hazelnuts

For the sauce

175ml/6fl oz double cream

seeds of 1 vanilla pod

100g/3½oz pink marshmallows

Hot choccy and churros

This makes me think of Valencia. After a particularly heavy night, which ended up in an open-air salsa club by the marina, I struggled round the corner to get a sugary fix of churros, the sweet donut-like icons, together with the sweetest, bestest hot chocolate in the history of the world (it was that big a hangover). So mark this page under 'hangover cure' and enjoy.

1 To make the churros, sift the flour, bicarbonate of soda and salt into a bowl. Make a well in the centre, add the water and whisk hard to combine and get rid of any lumps. Let the batter rest for 1 hour.

2 Heat the oil until a piece of bread sizzles when dropped in. Put the batter in a piping bag and squeeze down into the oil, cutting off after each 10cm/4inches of batter. Fry until golden brown, then drain on kitchen paper and roll the churros in sugar.

3 To make the hot choccy, put the chocolate in a bowl over barely simmering water (make sure the water doesn't touch the bottom of the bowl), and leave until melted.

4 Put the milk and cinnamon stick in a pan and warm for about 10 minutes. Meanwhile, whip the cream. Remove the cinnamon stick and whisk in the melted chocolate and the condensed milk until smooth. Pour into a mug, top with the whipped cream and drink with the churros.

For the churros

400g/14oz plain flour

1 tsp bicarbonate of soda

pinch of salt

400ml/14fl oz boiling water

vegetable oil for deep-frying

caster sugar for dusting

For the hot choccy

250g/9oz dark 70% cocoa-solids chocolate, broken into pieces

400ml/14fl oz milk

1 cinnamon stick

250ml/9fl oz condensed milk

225ml/8fl oz whipping cream

Chocolate and red wine pots
with donuts

Feeds 8

Even though we've got donuts with them, this is quite a grown-up taste, because of the wine in the choccy pots. The dessert is very rich, so don't serve these after a hugely stodgy meal, but if you do maybe make 16 mini pots and loads of tiny donuts.

1 First make the donuts. Cream the butter and sugar together in a bowl, add the eggs and beat well, then add a dash of vanilla extract and the milk.

2 In a separate bowl, mix the flour, polenta, baking powder and a pinch of salt. Add to the creamed ingredients and mix well. Sprinkle with flour, cover and chill for at least 8 hours.

3 To make the choccy pots, pour the wine into a pan, add 100g/3½oz of the sugar and bring to the boil. Simmer and reduce by two-thirds, then let it cool.

4 Melt the chocolate in a bowl over simmering water, then whisk in the wine syrup followed by the egg yolks.

5 Heat the milk, cream and remaining sugar in a pan to scalding point, then whisk into the chocolate mixture. Whisk in the butter, pour into eight ramekins and chill until set.

6 Turn out the donut dough onto a floured surface and roll out to 2cm/½inch thickness. Using a 5cm/2inch cutter, cut out loads of rounds. Put onto a board, sprinkle with flour and chill for 30 minutes.

7 Heat the oil and deep-fry the donuts until golden brown. Drain on kitchen paper, then roll them in sugar. Serve alongside the choccy pots with a quenelle of whipped cream, if you like.

For the donuts

75g/3oz unsalted butter, softened

75g/3oz caster sugar, plus extra to roll the donuts in

4 eggs

vanilla extract

2 tbsp milk

750g/1lb 11oz plain flour, plus extra for dusting

100g/3½oz dry polenta

2 tbsp baking powder

salt

vegetable oil for frying

For the choccy pots

250ml/9fl oz red wine, medium bodied and fruity

150g/5½oz caster sugar

500g/1lb 2oz dark 70% cocoa-solids chocolate, broken into pieces

8 egg yolks

275ml/9½fl oz milk

225ml/8fl oz double cream

15g/½oz unsalted butter

whipped cream, to serve (optional)

Strawberry
samosas

Feeds 6

These are good fun and great to serve after a curry. You can use any soft fruit
for the filling – mango also works particularly well. If you don't fancy them with
yoghurt, just drizzle with some honey.

1 To make the pastry, sift the flour and salt into a bowl, then 'cut' the butter into it until combined. Add the milk and form into a dough, then cover and chill for 20 minutes.

2 For the filling, put the strawberries into a bowl, add the lemon zest, sugar and cinnamon and stir to combine.

3 Roll out the pastry on a lightly floured surface and cut into six circles. Cut each circle in half and place a little of the strawberry mixture in one corner then fold over the opposite corner to make a tight triangle. Press down the edges to seal and brush with a little butter.

4 Heat the oil and shallow-fry the samosas until crisp and golden on all sides.

5 To make the yoghurt dressing, simply combine the yoghurt and mint in a bowl.

6 For the basil syrup, put the sugar, water and vanilla in a pan and heat until the sugar has dissolved. Allow to cool, then put in a food processor with the basil and blitz, then pass through a very fine sieve.

7 Serve a couple of samosas with a dollop of yoghurt dressing and a swirl of basil syrup.

225g/8oz plain flour, plus
extra for dusting
pinch of salt
25g/1oz unsalted butter, plus
extra for brushing
2 tbsp warm milk
vegetable oil for shallow frying

For the filling

225g/8oz strawberries, hulled and
chopped
zest of ½ lemon
50g/2oz soft light brown sugar
pinch of cinnamon

For the yoghurt dressing

175g/6oz Greek yoghurt
lots of freshly chopped mint

For the basil syrup

200g/7oz caster sugar
150ml/5fl oz water
splash of vanilla extract
lots of fresh basil leaves

Bounty profiteroles

Feeds 6–8

I like to serve one large profiterole, which is probably really a choux bun, but you can do lots of little ones if you like. Oh, before you start this, you have to make the custard for the filling a day in advance – so none until tomorrow, then.

1 First make the filling. Whisk the egg yolks and sugar in a bowl until pale and fluffy, then sift in the flour and mix well. Pour the coconut milk into a pan and bring to the boil. As soon as it boils, pour it onto the egg mixture and stir well. Pour it back into the pan and bring back to the boil, then turn down the heat and cook for another 5 minutes until it thickens. Spoon it back into a bowl and fold in the desiccated coconut, then cover and chill overnight. Make sure the clingfilm is resting on the surface so you don't get a skin.

2 The next day, whip the cream and fold into the custard.

3 To make the choux buns, preheat the oven to 200°C/400°F/mark 6. Put the butter and water into a pan, bring to the boil and heat until the butter melts. Take the pan off the heat, tip in all the flour and mix well. Using a wooden spoon, beat in the eggs, one at a time. Add a pinch of salt.

4 Transfer the dough to a piping bag and allow to cool for a few minutes. Now pipe 'blobs' of pastry onto a floured baking tray. You'll get about 8 squash or golfball size dollops, or as many little ones as you like. The thing to remember is that the pastry will at least double in size, so give them plenty of space on the sheet to expand.

5 Bake in the oven for 30–40 minutes. You want them golden and firm on the outside and dry in the middle. I quite often put them on the bottom shelf for another 5–10 minutes to make sure.

6 To make the sauce, simply heat the ingredients together in a saucepan until combined.

7 Make a small hole in the base of each profiterole and pipe in some custard. Then sit it in the middle of a plate and pour over some warm choccy sauce. I think this is where I say it's a taste of paradise.

150g/5½oz unsalted butter
225ml/8fl oz water
225g/8oz plain flour, plus extra for dusting
6 eggs
pinch of salt

For the filling

6 egg yolks
125g/4½oz caster sugar
40g/1½oz plain flour
400ml tin of coconut milk
50g/2oz desiccated coconut
200ml/7fl oz double cream

For the sauce

200g/7oz dark 70% cocoa-solids chocolate, broken into pieces
50g/2oz unsalted butter
150ml/5fl oz water

Winter fruit clafoutis

Feeds 6

Sometimes winter fruits can be a bit temperamental, which is why crumbles and pies are good options. Another option is this clafoutis, which is basically fruit soaked in booze, topped with a sweet batter and baked. Of course, you can use summer fruits as well.

1 Put the fruit into a bowl, sprinkle the Malibu over and leave for 30 minutes.

2 Preheat the oven to 200°C/400°F/mark 6. Put the milk, cream and vanilla seeds in a pan and bring to the boil. Take off the heat and cool slightly.

3 Put the sugar and eggs into a bowl and beat well, then add the flour and salt and stir to mix.

4 Strain in the milk mixture and beat well.

5 Butter a 23 x 25cm/9 x 10inch dish and sprinkle with sugar. Add the fruit, then pour the batter over.

6 Bake in the oven for 25 minutes, then leave to cool. Serve with lightly whipped cream.

450g/1lb prepared winter fruits, such as cranberry, pear, apple

4 tbsp Malibu coconut liqueur

100ml/3½fl oz milk

150ml/5fl oz whipping cream, plus extra to serve

seeds from 1 vanilla pod

150g caster sugar, plus extra for sprinkling

4 eggs

25g/1oz plain flour

pinch of salt

butter for greasing

Blueberry pancakes

Feeds 4–6

Now the cottage cheese in the mixture is wonderful. I started using it because one of my fave authors, Robert Crais, has a detective character called Elvis Cole, who uses cottage cheese in his pancake mix, so I tried it and it works – see what you learn from books.

1 Mix the flour, bicarbonate of soda and sugar together in a bowl.

2 In a separate bowl, combine the egg, melted butter, milk and cottage cheese, then stir into the flour mix. Stir in the blueberries and lemon zest.

3 Spoon some of the mixture into a lightly oiled warm frying pan and cook for 1 minute on each side, until golden. Continue to make pancakes in the same way with the remaining mixture.

4 Sit a few pancakes in a stack and drizzle maple syrup over the top.

200g/7oz self-raising flour

1 tsp bicarbonate of soda

50g/2oz caster sugar

1 egg

50g/2oz unsalted butter, melted

250ml/9fl oz milk

125g/4½oz cottage cheese

225g/8oz blueberries

zest of 1 small lemon

vegetable oil for frying

maple syrup, to serve

Banana tarte tatin

I remember sitting in a café in Paris eating warm apple tatin and a brandy with Ali, my wife, and thinking all was right with the world. That's how tatin makes you feel; it's warming, comforting and scrummy – but I prefer dark rum to brandy and bananas go better with my tipple, so I wait for the day when it's banana tatin and rum in a café in Jamaica – 'til then Chorlton will have to do.

1 Preheat the oven to 190ºC/375ºF/mark 5. Pour the water into a heavy-bottomed pan, sprinkle over the sugar and heat, without stirring, until the sugar dissolves, then simmer gently until the sugar turns golden. Stir in the butter, then pour into a 18cm/7inch round baking tin.

2 Pack the banana pieces tightly into the tin.

3 Press the pastry over the top of the bananas and trim, then bake for about 20 minutes, until the pastry is crisp and golden.

4 Allow to cool until just warm, then turn out and serve with clotted cream.

50ml/2fl oz water

100g/3½oz caster sugar

25g/1oz unsalted butter

12 bananas, peeled and cut into 5cm/2inch pieces

200g/7oz ready-rolled puff pastry

clotted cream, to serve

Rosemary and olive oil cake with honeyed figs

Feeds 8

You know when you fancy a bit of cake with your tea or coffee in the afternoon, but you don't want a sticky gooey beast? Well, this Italian cake hits the spot. It's sweet enough to give a boost and a treat, but doesn't overface you. However, if you serve it with the honeyed figs and black pepper ricotta, you're asking for trouble.

1 Preheat the oven to 170ºC/325ºF/mark 3. Put the eggs and sugar into a food processor and whiz until pale and fluffy.

2 Keep the motor running and drizzle in the oil, then with the mixer on slow add the flour, baking powder and salt and pulse to incorporate. Turn out into a bowl and fold in the rosemary.

3 Pour into a 25cm/10inch greased loaf tin and bake in the oven for 45–50 minutes. Cool, then turn out.

4 For the figs, put the marsala and honey in a small pan and bring to the boil, then quickly coat the figs.

5 For the ricotta, put all the ingredients into a bowl and stir to mix.

6 Serve slices of the cake with the figs, ricotta and a glass of vin santo.

4 eggs

150g/5½oz caster sugar

125ml/4fl oz extra-virgin olive oil

300g/10½oz plain flour

1 tbsp baking powder

pinch of salt

finely chopped fresh rosemary, to taste

butter for greasing

For the honeyed figs

50ml/2fl oz marsala wine

50g/2oz honey

6 figs, halved

For the ricotta

100g/3½oz ricotta cheese

100ml/3½fl oz whipped cream

25g/1oz caster sugar

black pepper

Lemon, lime and orange polenta cake

Feeds 10–12

I don't know why this is so gorgeous. I'm not a huge fan of polenta and I'm not a huge fan of 'plain' cakes, but this little number with a cup of tea or coffee is divine. It's so moist – traditionally it's done with just lemon, but I love that Opal Fruit effect of all three citrus fruits. It's also the kind of cake that cake tins were invented for.

1 Preheat the oven to 180ºC/350ºF/mark 4. Cream the butter and sugar in a bowl until pale and fluffy, then stir in the almonds.

2 Add the eggs, one at a time, then the vanilla.

3 Stir in the zests and juices, then mix in the polenta, salt and baking powder.

4 Spoon the mixture into a 30cm/12inch greased and floured cake tin and bake for 45–55 minutes until golden and firm. Leave to cool in the tin.

5 Serve on its own or with some mascarpone – and tea or coffee.

450g/1lb unsalted butter, plus extra for greasing

450g/1lb caster sugar

450g/1lb ground almonds

6 eggs

good dash of vanilla extract

zest of 2 lemons, 1 orange and 1 lime

juice of ½ lemon and ½ lime

a quick squeeze of orange juice

225g/8oz polenta

pinch of salt

1½ tsp baking powder

flour for dusting

Index